PICTORIAL ANATOMY OF THE FROG

ILLUSTRATIONS AND TEXT BY STEPHEN G. GILBERT

UNIVERSITY OF WASHINGTON PRESS

SEATTLE · 1965

Copyright © 1965 by the University of Washington Press

Library of Congress Catalog Card Number 65-14843

Printed in the United States of America

Preface

This book is designed to serve as a guide to the recognition of anatomical structures encountered in the dissection of the frog, and also as a permanent record of structures and relations which are necessarily destroyed in the course of the work. The brief text is not intended as a substitute for a standard, full-length treatment, but rather to emphasize the connection between form and function and to suggest further reading for those interested. Most of the text is based on the works by Holmes, Marshall, Noble, and Ecker cited in the bibliography, and readers interested in a complete written description of the anatomy of the frog should refer to those sources.

Except for the illustration of the inner ear on page 51 (which is after a drawing of Retzius reproduced by Ecker), the illustrations are all original and were drawn, unless otherwise noted, from dissections of the bullfrog, *Rana catesbeiana*. The remarks in the text apply to ranid frogs in general. In the case of the muscles and in most other instances the nomenclature adopted by Holmes has been followed.

I would like to thank Dr. Richard C. Snyder of the University of Washington, who generously checked the drawings and the text and made many helpful suggestions; Dr. Hobart M. Smith of the University of Illinois, who read and criticized the text; and Dr. James Kezer of the University of Oregon, who provided me with instruments and specimens for some of the work.

I would also like to thank the following publishers for permission to use the material indicated:

The illustration of the nervous system on page 48 and the illustrations of ovulation and tadpole development on pages 45, 46, and 47 were originally done for a laboratory manual by Dr. James Kezer and are used by his permission and by permission of the publishers, the Burgess Publishing Company of Minneapolis, Minnesota.

The drawings of the bullfrog seizing its prey on page 27 are based on photos by M. F. Roberts published in "A Bullfrog and its Prey" by Carl Gans (*Natural History*, Vol. LXX), No. 2, reproduced by permission of *Natural History Magazine*.

The drawings of the pond frogs and the spring peepers on pages 54 and 61 are based on photos published in *Living Amphibians of the World* by Doris M. Cochran (Garden City, New York: Doubleday & Co., 1961), by permission of the Chanticleer Press.

STEPHEN G. GILBERT

Contents

PICTORIAL ANATOMY OF THE FROG

The common European frog, *Rana temporaria,* as it appeared on the cover of Ecker's *Anatomie des Frosches.* (By permission of the Clarendon Press, Oxford.)

I would on first setting out, inform the reader that there is a much greater number of miracles and natural secrets in the frog than anyone hath ever before thought of or discovered.

Swammerdam

Historical Introduction

Frogs have been a favorite subject for experiment since the beginning of the scientific study of biology. Their wide distribution and the relative ease with which they may be kept in captivity have made them easily accessible to scientists, and their remarkable capacity for surviving experimental operations makes them suitable for many demonstrations and investigations which could not be performed on warm-blooded animals due to the danger from shock, loss of blood, and infection. Frogs have probably been the subject of more experimental investigations than any other laboratory animal, and their anatomy has been described more fully (in Alexander Ecker and Robert Wiedersheim's *Anatomie des Frosches*) than that of any other animal except man. Their popularity among scientists led Ecker, in the introduction to his classic work on the frog, to remark that they enjoyed the dubious honor of being the official "domestic animal of the physiologist."

"These unfortunate batrachians," said Ecker, "have now fallen into the hands of a more terrible master than the stork of the fable, and their prophetic cry in Aristophanes' choir of frogs, 'We will have yet more terrible things to endure,' has been richly fulfilled."

One cannot read far in the history of biology without coming upon descriptions of basic physiological experiments and discoveries in which the frog has served as the chief subject, and therefore brief descriptions of a few of the more important discoveries made with the help of the frog may be of interest to readers with a taste for history and also serve to illustrate some of the reasons for the widespread use of the frog in modern laboratories and classrooms.

The English physician William Harvey (1578-1657) observed that frogs were particularly well suited to his studies of the heart because "these things [motions of the heart] are more obvious in the colder animals, such as toads [and] frogs . . ."[1] The publication in 1628 of Harvey's *Anatomical Dissertation Concerning the Motion of the Heart and Blood in Animals* is often said to mark the beginning of the scientific study of biology. In this work Harvey set forth his theory that blood does not ebb and flow as Galen had taught, but follows a continuous circuit, flowing away from the heart in the arteries and toward it in the veins.

Harvey did his work before compound microscopes were in general use, and was therefore unable to discover the capillaries through which blood passes from the arteries to the veins. He could only say that the blood "is sent for distribution to all parts of the body, where it makes its way into the veins and pores of the flesh, and then flows by the veins from the circumference on every side to the centre."[1] He did not believe in the existence of capillaries connecting the arteries and the veins. In 1651 he wrote:

> I confess, I say, nay, I even pointedly assert, that I have never found any visible anastomoses . . . [between arteries and veins]. Even in a dead animal it [blood] falls of its own accord through the finest pores of the flesh and skin from superior into inferior parts.[2]

It was Marcello Malpighi, the Italian anatomist and botanist (1628-1694), who used the microscope to discover the capillaries connecting arteries and veins. He was born in 1628, the same year in which Harvey's work was published. Malpighi made numerous discoveries with the aid of the microscope, among them the stomata of leaves,

3

the Malpighian bodies of the kidney, and the tracheal and Malpighian tubes of insects.

In 1661 Malpighi reported his observations on the lung of the frog, which he made with a view to discovering "whether the vessels of the lung are connected by anastomoses, or gape into the common substance of the lungs and sinuses." He says:

I had believed that this body of the blood breaks into the empty space, and is collected again by a gaping vessel and by the structure of the walls. The tortuous and diffuse motion of the blood in divers directions, and its union at a determined place offered a handle to this. But the dried lung of the frog made my belief dubious. This lung had, by chance, preserved the red-

ness of the blood in (what afterwards proved to be) the smallest vessels, where by means of a more perfect lens, no more met the eye the points forming the skin called *Sagrino* [superficial nodules], but vessels mingled annularly. And, so great is the divarication of these vessels as they go out, here from a vein, there from an artery, that order is no longer preserved, but a network appears made up of the prolongations of both vessels. . . . Here it was clear to sense that the blood flows away thru the tortuous vessels, that it is not poured into spaces but always works thru tubules, and is dispersed by the multiple windings of the vessels.[3]

The work of Harvey and Malpighi in explaining the anatomy and mechanics of the pulmonary circulation was followed toward the end of the seventeenth century by experiments on respiration by Robert Boyle and other members of the Royal Society. One widely held contemporary theory related by Boyle was that the "genuine use" of respiration was ". . . ventilation . . . of the blood, in its passage through the lungs; in which passage it is disburthened of those excrementitious steams preceding for the most part, from the superfluous serosities of the blood and of the chyle too, which . . . hath been newly mixed with it in the heart."[4] Another member of the Royal Society, Lower, showed that the dark blood taken from a vein becomes bright red on being shaken with air, and concluded that the change was due to "the particles of air insinuating themselves into the blood."[5] Other members of the same group performed experiments which suggested a connection between respiration and combustion. However, other theories of respiration were current at the time, and even in the mid-eighteenth century a commonly used text (Haller's *Elements of Physiology*) described breathing as a process which aided the circulation of the blood by compressing it in the abdomen and thus forcing it into the heart and arteries more rapidly. It was not until the latter part of the eighteenth century that Priestley discovered the ability of plants to effect the "restoration of air infected with animal respiration."[6] Within a few years of Priestley's experiments, Ingen-Housz made his pioneering studies of photosynthesis and the identity of respiration and combustion was demonstrated by Lavoisier.

The Dutch physician, naturalist, and microscopist Jan Swammerdam (1637-1680) saw the capillaries of the frog's lung about the same time Malpighi saw them, but Swammerdam's observations were not published until 1737. His beautiful *Biblia Naturae* includes an anatomical description

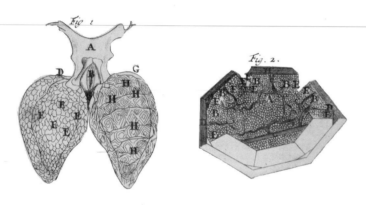

Malpighi's drawings of the lungs of the frog. His captions are:

FIG. I. Showing lungs of frogs with trachea attached. (A) Larynx, which is semicartilaginous. (B) Rima, which is accurately closed and opened at the animal's need. Air being enclosed, it keeps the lungs expanded. (C) Site of the heart. (D) External part of the lung. (E) Prolonged *rete* of the cells. (F) Prolongation of the pulmonary artery. (G) Concave part of the lung divided through the middle. (H) Prolongation of the pulmonary vein running through the apices.

FIG II. Containing the most simple cell without the intermediate walls (magnified). (A) Interior floor of the cell. (B) Parietes separated and bent. (C) Trunk of pulmonary artery with attached branches, as if ending in a network. (D) Trunk of pulmonary vein wandering with its branches over the slopes of the walls. (E) Vessel in the bottom and corners of the walls with the ramifications of the *rete* continued. From Marcello Malpighi's *De Pulmonibus Epistola Altera*, Bononia, 1661. (Courtesy of the Library of the New York Academy of Medicine.)

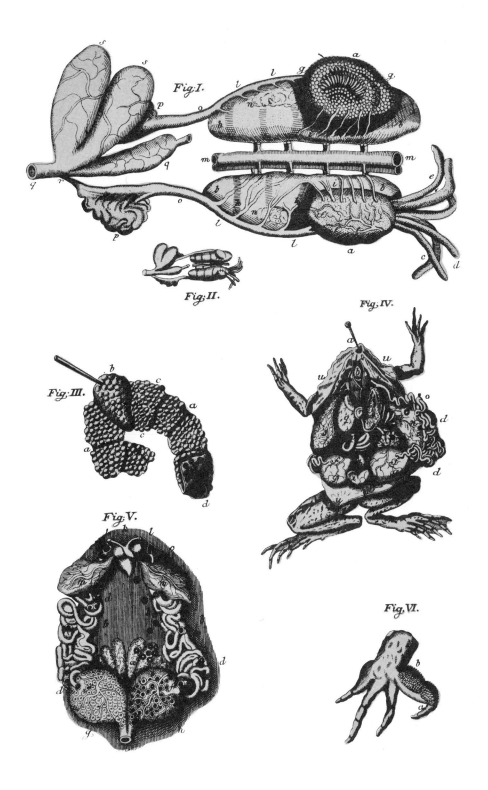

Swammerdam's drawings of frog dissections. His caption is:

FIG. I: The genitals of the male frog, viewed with the microscope.

FIG. II: All of the foregoing parts, of their natural size.

FIG. III: One of the ovaries, of its natural size.

FIG. IV: The heart, liver, lungs, tubes, uterus, etc., in an impregnated frog.

FIG. V: The manner of finding the eggs dispersed in the frog's belly, when in their passage through the tube into the uterus.

FIG. VI: A microscopical view of the forelegs or arms of the male frog. From Jan Swammerdam's *Book of Nature*. London: C. G. Seyffert, 1758. (Courtesy of the Oregon State University Library.)

of the frog and observations on the development of the frog's egg.

Swammerdam describes experiments in which he used frogs as subjects for the study of nerve and muscle action. One contemporary theory held that muscular contraction was caused by "subtle fluids" or "animal spirits" which flowed through the nerves, causing inflation of the muscles. Swammerdam countered this argument by devising an ingenious experiment in which he used the muscle of a frog to demonstrate that there is no increase in volume when a muscle contracts. He concluded that "we should . . . reject that opinion which supposes a spirituous matter to be necessary to excite muscular motion, and that it flows out of the brain."[6] Muscular contraction, he said, was not due to any kind of "inflation, fermentation, or explosive motion."[7]

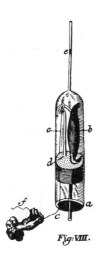

Fig. VIII.

Swammerdam's illustration of one of his experiments. The fact that the drop of water (e) did not rise when he caused the muscle to contract by stimulating the nerve showed that there was no increase in the volume of the muscle during contraction. From Jan Swammerdam's *Book of Nature.* London: C. G. Seyffert, 1758. (Courtesy of the Oregon State University Library.)

Observing that physical, chemical, or thermal stimulation of a nerve resulted in muscular contraction even though the nerve was cut, he wrote: "Muscular motion does not seem to require in any animal, any other communication between the nerve and the muscle than a bare commotion of the nerve by any cause whatsoever."[7] He elaborated his theory as follows:

In order to further explain the origin of this natural and perpetual contraction of the muscles; I think indeed it arises from the continual impulse of the arterial blood upon the marrow [spinal cord] and nerves; for, by means of this blood, all those parts seem to be continually moved, excited, and irritated to convey that motion perpetually and uniformly to the muscles, and to prepare the latter for their perpetual contraction. For this reason, all the nerves without exception, have not fewer arteries in proportion, than the brain itself, and the spinal marrow have.[7]

At the beginning of his chapter on muscle action, Swammerdam remarks:

As to myself, I candidly confess, that I have not brought every subject, which I have advanced, to the greatest possible perfection; for, in order to attain this, I should have spent my whole life discovering one thing, and this course is not agreeable to me; for I am thoroughly persuaded that, if I came to the utmost extremity, I should at last discover nothing but my own ignorance.[7]

Had Swammerdam continued his studies on nerve and muscle action he might have discovered that a weak electrical stimulus applied to the nerve could cause muscular contraction. But his wide-ranging interests led him into other fields, leaving this discovery to Luigi Galvani.

Swammerdam's elaborate drawings and descriptions provide a fascinating insight into the long processes of discovery which lie behind many anatomical and physiological details recited in contemporary texts. An English edition of his book, published in 1758, should be of great interest to those wishing to read in the history of biology.

The first recorded observation of the capillaries in the gills of the tadpole is found in a letter dated September 7, 1688, which was written by the Dutch microscopist and anatomist Anton van Leeuwenhoek (1632-1723). He writes:

These parts (the external gills) alone caused me to have the tadpole drawn: for in each of these parts I saw to my great amusement very clearly the circulation of the blood, which was pushed along from the parts nearest to the body to those farthest away from it, thus performing a continuous very swift circulation. The blood did not circulate smoothly, for in a very short time it was again driven along, and continually so; and before this very quick impulse took place, we should have thought that a standstill in the circulation would have followed if we had not seen a continual progress in the course of the blood. But hardly had a movement of the blood slowed down, when another very quick impulse followed: hence a continuous circulation took place in the blood of this animal. And if I try accurately to measure the short time between each of these impulses, I must say that in the time a rapid tongue could hardly count up to a hundred, there were as many as a hundred quick impulses of the blood. From this I concluded that an equal number of times the blood was driven from the heart. And so distinctly was this movement of the blood being driven from the heart and the transition of the arteries into the veins, as neither myself nor anyone else could imagine.[2]

Leeuwenhoek traced the circulation farther from the aorta to the postcava and wrote:

This proved to me that the blood vessels we see in this animal and which we call arteries and veins are one and the same blood vessels; they can be called arteries only so long as they carry the blood to the farthest parts of the small blood vessels, and veins when they carry the blood to the heart again. . . . Though we have now had the great fortune (to which we have been looking forward and which we have ever been seeking in vain) to show clearly the circulation of the blood and its passing from the arteries into the veins in the above-mentioned frog and fishes, yet we shall not rest, but do our duty also to examine other animals and, if possible, detect the same things in them.[2]

Leeuwenhoek and Malpighi both described red blood corpuscles in the blood of the frog, and Leeuwenhoek observed and illustrated the spermatozoa of the frog.

Leeuwenhoek's illustration of the tadpole, from his letter of September 7, 1688. (Courtesy of the Library of the New York Academy of Medicine.)

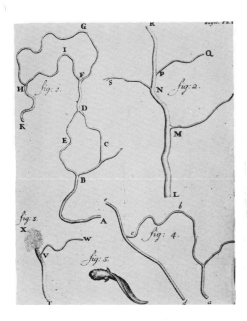

Leeuwenhoek's illustration of capillaries in the tadpole, from his letter of September 25, 1699. He wrote: "The motion of the blood in these tadpoles exceeds all the rest of small animals, and fish, I have seen; nay, this pleasure has oftentimes been so recreating to me, that I do not believe that all the pleasure of fountains or waterworks, either natural or made by art, could have pleased my sight so well, as the view of these creatures have given me." (Courtesy of the Library of the New York Academy of Medicine.)

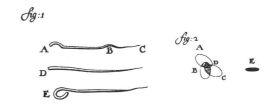

Leeuwenhoek's illustrations of the spermatozoa (fig. 1) and the erythrocytes (fig. 2) of the frog. From his letter of July 16, 1683, as reproduced in *The Collected Letters of Antoni van Leeuwenhoek*, Vol. IV. Amsterdam: Swets & Zeitlinger, Ltd., 1952. By permission of Swets & Zeitlinger, Ltd.

Some of Galvani's experiments as illustrated in his *De Viribus Electricitatis in Motu Musculari Commentarius* (Commentary on the Effect of Electricity on Muscular Motion), 1792. (Courtesy of the Yale University Historical Library.)

Another discovery of pivotal importance was made by an Italian physician, Luigi Galvani (1737-1798), whose experiments on the frog led to the discovery of the principle of the electric battery and to studies on the electrical nature of the nervous impulse. Until the time of Galvani's work (about 1786) a continuous electrical current had never been generated by man. Those who studied electrical phenomena had experimented with magnets and with the shocks, attractions, and repulsions produced by static electricity machines, but descriptions of these phenomena were for the most part qualitative rather than quantitative. It was only about thirty years before Galvani's

experiment that Benjamin Franklin had demonstrated the "sameness of electric matter with that of lightning," a "sameness" by no means obvious to Franklin's contemporaries.

Galvani describes his original observation in these words:

I had dissected and prepared a frog . . . and while I was attending to something else, I laid it on a table on which stood an electrical machine at some distance. . . . Now when one of the persons who were present touched accidentally and lightly the inner crural nerves of the frog with the point of a scalpel all the muscles of the legs seemed to contract again and again. . . . Another one who was there, who was helping us in electrical researches, thought that he had noticed that the action was excited when a spark was discharged from the conductor of the machine. Being astonished by this new phenomenon he called my attention to it, who at that time had something else in mind and was deep in

thought. Whereupon I was inflamed with an incredible zeal and eagerness to test the same and to bring to light what was concealed in it.[8]

Curious to know whether lightning would produce the same result as the spark from the static electricity machine, Galvani tied a wire to the leg of a frog and led the wire to a well. Touching the frog with another wire attached to a metallic conductor on top of his house, he observed:

As often as the lightning broke forth, the muscles were thrown into repeated violent convulsions, so that always, as the lightning lightened the sky, the muscle contractions and movements preceded the thunder and, as it were, announced its coming. It was best, however, when the lightning was strong or the clouds from which it broke forth were near the place of the experiment.[9]

Galvani devised numerous experiments in the course of which he discovered that muscular contractions also occurred if the leg and the spinal cord were touched with a bow made of two different metals. He wrote:

These (muscular contractions) occur more clearly and more quickly not only with one but with two curved rods, if they are so applied and arranged that the end of one of them touches the muscle and the end of the other the nerves in a similar way, and the other two ends are brought in contact with each other. . . . Furthermore we were fortunate enough to observe this peculiar and remarkable phenomenon, that the use of more than one metallic substance and the differences between them contribute much to the excitation, as also especially to the increase of the muscular contraction, far more indeed than when one and the same metal is used. Thus for example, if the whole rod was iron . . . the contractions either did not occur or were very small. But if one of them was iron and the other brass, or better if it was silver (silver seems to us the best of all the metals for conducting animal electricity) there occur repeated and much greater and more prolonged contractions.[8]

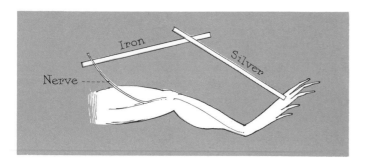

The principle of Galvani's experiment: When the leg and the nerve are touched with a bow made of two different metals, muscular contractions occur.

Galvani tried touching the leg and the nerve simultaneously with nonconductors such as "glass, rubber, resin, stone or wood, . . ." and reported:

> With these nothing similar occurred, no muscular contractions and motions could be seen. Naturally such a result excited in us no slight astonishment and caused us to think that possibly the electricity was present in the animal itself. We were confirmed in this view by the assumption of a very fine nervous fluid which during the occurrence of the phenomenon flows from the nerves to the muscle like the electric current in the Leyden jar.[8]

Galvani did not understand that the two different metals, together with the frog's leg, generated a weak electric current and that the leg acted as a sensitive detector of this current. Because the contractions could be elicited without a known source of electricity outside the frog, and because the contractions did not occur when a nonconductor was placed between the nerve and the muscle, Galvani thought that the contractions were caused by electricity originating within the nervous system of the frog and "short-circuited" by the metal bow.

The definitive tests which showed Galvani's interpretation to be in error were made by the Italian physicist Alessandro Volta (1745-1827). Using a sensitive condensing electrometer of his own invention, he showed that no electricity could be detected in animal tissues. He then showed that a weak current could be detected between two different metals separated by brine-soaked paper. He concluded that the muscular contractions observed by Galvani were not the result of animal electricity but were "really the effects of a very feeble artificial electricity, which is generated in a way that is beyond doubt by the simple application of two metals."[9] In 1792 he wrote:

> By this time I am persuaded that the electric fluid is never excited and moved by the proper action of the organs, or by any vital force, or extended to be brought from one part of the animal to another, but that it is determined and constrained by virtue of the impulse which it receives in the place where the metals join.

Galvani never accepted this explanation; he died in 1798 after several years of futile controversy with Volta. By 1800 Volta had developed the Voltaic pile, or battery, by using metals separated by pieces of pasteboard soaked in brine, and a new era of electrical experiment and invention was beginning.

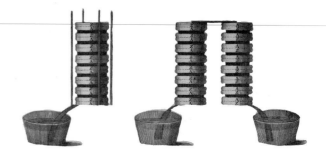

One of Volta's arrangements for producing a continuous flow of electricity was a series of zinc and silver plates separated by brine-soaked paper. From Alessandro Volta's "On the Electricity Excited by the Mere Contact of Conducting Substances of Different Kinds," in *The Philosophical Transactions of the Royal Society of London, 1800.* (Courtesy of the Library of the New York Academy of Medicine.)

Although Galvani's interpretation of his observations was incorrect, his work was widely read and gave rise to numerous experiments by other scientists who were eager to devise new methods by which nerve and muscle reactions could be tested with galvanic stimuli. The relatively simple facts of nerve and muscle physiology which were known at the end of the eighteenth century could be experimentally demonstrated in less than half an hour. However, with the beginning of the nineteenth century, physiological investigation was stimulated by a number of factors, including the electrical discoveries which followed Galvani's work, improvements in the microscope due to the introduction of achromatic lenses, discoveries in comparative and descriptive anatomy, and evolutionary speculation.

Among the nineteenth-century scientists who employed galvanic stimuli was the great German physiologist Johannes Mueller (1801-1858). One of his most famous contributions is the following demonstration, published in 1833, of the functions of the dorsal and ventral roots of the spinal nerves of the frog. He writes:

Sir Charles Bell first conceived the ingenious idea that the dorsal roots of the spinal nerves, which have upon them a ganglion, are the source of sensation, whereas the ventral roots are the source of motion; and that the primitive fibers of these roots after their union are mingled in one trunk, and thus distributed for the supply of the skin and muscles.

Mueller then refers to work by Magendie and a number of other men who attempted to confirm Bell's theory experimentally. The operations, however, caused such severe shock in higher vertebrates that most of the animals died before decisive results could be obtained. Mueller continues:

The happy thought at length occurred to me of performing the experiment on frogs. These animals are very tenacious of life, and long survive the opening of the vertebral canal. In them, also, the nerves retain their excitability for a very considerable time, and the large roots of the nerves of the posterior extremities run a long distance within the cavtiy of the spine before uniting.

Mueller opened the vertebral column and cut the dorsal root of a spinal nerve going to the hind leg. He continues:

The cord of one of the dorsal roots being now seized with a pair of forceps and the root itself irritated repeatedly with the point of the needle, not the slightest contraction of the muscles of the posterior extremities ever ensues. . . .

One of the ventral roots of the nerves of the lower extremity, which are equally as large as the dorsal, is now raised with the needle out of the vertebral canal, and it is found that the slightest touch of the ventral roots excites the most powerful contractions of the whole limb. Having cut them through at their insertion into the cord, the extremity of one is seized with the forceps, and the needle is used to irritate it as in the case of the dorsal root. Each time the point of the needle is applied, most distinct twitchings of the muscles take place. . . . I may further remark that the section of the dorsal roots is frequently attended with very distinct manifestations of the sensation of pain in the anterior part of the body. . . .

Equally decisive results were obtained by the application of galvanic stimuli with simple copper and zinc plates.

Mueller described the nervous impulse as an "imponderable psychical principle" whose velocity could not be measured. Yet within less than

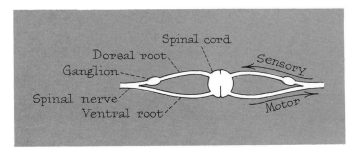

The principle of Mueller's experiment: Each spinal nerve is attached to the spinal cord by a dorsal and a ventral root. Stimulation of the dorsal root produces manifestations of pain, but no muscular contractions. Stimulation of the ventral root is followed by muscular contractions. The interpretation of this and related experiments is that sensory impulses are carried by the dorsal root and that motor impulses are carried by the ventral root.

twenty years after his demonstration of the function of the spinal nerve roots, one of Mueller's students, Hermann von Helmholtz (1821-1894), succeeded in measuring the speed of the nervous impulse in a frog's leg.

Helmholtz prepared the leg so that the sciatic nerve could be stimulated by two electrodes placed very close together on the nerve. A pen attached to the leg recorded the contractions as a curve on a rapidly revolving cylinder. Helmholtz writes:

Now, if we arrange for two curves to be drawn in succession, and if we take care that at the moment of stimulation the pen occupies always exactly the same point on the surface [of the cylinder], then both curves will have the same starting point, and from the congruence or noncongruence of their individual parts one can observe whether or not different stages of the mechanical muscle response have occurred, in both instances, at the same or a later time after stimulation.

He stimulated the nerve at two different points, one near the muscle and one farther from the muscle, and observed:

. . . each drawing consists of two curves of congruent shape which are shifted in a horizontal direction with respect to each other by a certain amount . . . such that the curve which has been drawn upon stimulation of the nearer nerve spot, is also nearer to the starting point of stimulation.[11]

By calculating the time represented by the displacement of the two curves and comparing it with the distance between the two points of stimulation on the nerve, Helmholtz estimated the speed of the nervous impulse in the sciatic nerve of the frog to be 27.25 meters per second (about 60 miles per hour).

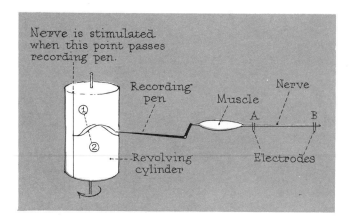

The principle of Helmholtz' experiment: Tracing #1 is the record of stimulation at point A; tracing #2 is the record of stimulation at point B. The displacement of the two tracings is due to the fact that it takes slightly longer for the nervous impulse to reach the muscle from B than A.

Helmholtz illustrated his apparatus for measuring the speed of the nervous impulse with this engraving. From Hermann von Helmholtz' *"Messungen ueber Fortpflanzungsgeschwindigkeit der Reizung in den Nerven,"* in *Archiv fur Anatomie, Physiologie, und wissenschaftliche Medizin,* 1852. (Courtesy of the Library of the New York Academy of Medicine.)

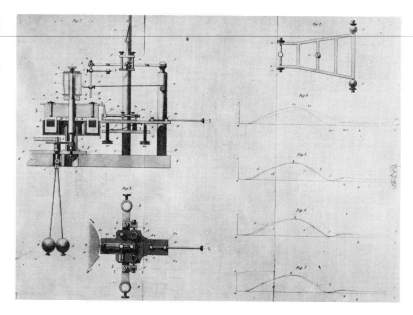

In 1864 the first edition of Ecker's *Anatomie des Frosches* was published by Vieweg and Son of Braunschweig. It was the first time an entire book had been devoted to the anatomy of the frog. In his introduction to the first edition, Ecker mentions the work of Leeuwenhoek, Swammerdam, Galvani, and Mueller, and gives the following summary of other important work which had been done on the frog up to that time:

. . . an accurate acquaintance with the constituents of the blood directly concerned in nutrition has been obtained by observation on the frog, as well as important facts in the physiology of the blood and lymph, such as the intimate knowledge of the corpuscles of both fluids, and the coagulability of the plasma; while in no less degree have experiments on these animals served to establish the laws of the heart's action. Moreover, physiology is not the only science indebted to the frog: in histology many important results have been obtained from observations on it, and for histological instruction it is now indispensable. To it we owe much of our knowledge of the structure of nerve fibers, their origin and termination, especially in muscle, their relations within the ganglia, and even the structure of the muscle fiber itself. For the study of reproduction and development the frog has, next to the chick, afforded the most important material: one need but refer to the investigations on impregnation from the time of Spallanzani to that of Newport, the phenomena of cleavage, and many others.[12]

Ecker goes on to remark that although the frog is widely used as an experimental subject

> . . . the literature of the anatomy of the frog is so widely scattered in monographs and journals that reference to it involves the expenditure of much time. This attempt . . . to produce a complete anatomy of the frog based throughout upon my own observations cannot be considered superfluous.[12]

In 1889 an English edition of Ecker's book, translated and annotated by George Haslam, was published by the Clarendon Press, Oxford. In 1894 Vieweg and Son asked the anatomist Ernst Gaupp to prepare a revised edition of Ecker's work. The popularity of the book at that time can be judged by Gaupp's remark in the preface to the revised edition to the effect that Ecker's book had become as indispensable to anatomists, physiologists, and zoologists as the frog itself. Gaupp completely revised Ecker's work, adding many original observations and including information from papers which had appeared since the first edition was published. His revision was so complete that the book grew to several times its original size. The revised edition, published between 1896 and 1904, is more than 1700 pages long. In spite of the apparent exhaustiveness of Gaupp's account, he often ends a section with the comment that he has presented only a brief and provisional discussion which will have to await further research for definitive treatment. Even a brief look at Gaupp's revision of Ecker's book provides an insight into the tremendous amount of work which had been done on the frog by 1904, an insight which may be missed by those who confine their reading to the necessarily brief remarks in zoology texts.

In spite of the innumerable studies which have been made on the frog, modern refinements in equipment and techniques are continually opening new fields of inquiry and each year sees an increase in the number of scientific papers dealing with experiments performed on the frog. Nevertheless, many fundamental questions are still unanswered, and there is no doubt that frogs will continue to provide material for experimental investigation as long as biology is studied.

NOTES

1. Harvey, William. *Excercitatio Anatomica de Motu Cordis et Sanguinis in Animalibus.* Frankfurt, 1628. Translated by Robert Willis and quoted in: Schwartz, George, and Philip W. Bishop. Moments of Discovery. New York: Basic Books, Inc., 1958.

2. Schierbeek, A. *Measuring the Invisible World.* New York: Abelard-Schuman Ltd., 1959. By permission of Abelard-Schuman, Ltd.

3. Malpighi, Marcello. *De Pulmonibus Epistola Altera.* Bononia, 1661. Translated by James Young in the *Proceedings of the Royal Society of Medicine,* Vol. 23, No. 1, Nov. 1929. By permission of the Royal Society of Medicine.

4. Boyle, Robert. *New Experiments Physicomechanical Touching the Spring of the Air and Its Effects Made for the Most Part in a New Pneumatical Engine.* Oxford, 1660. Quoted in: Hall, Thomas S. A Source Book in Animal Biology. New York: McGraw-Hill Book Co., Inc. 1951.

5. Hogben, Lancelot. *Science for The Citizen.* New York: Alfred A. Knopf, 1938.

6. Priestley, Joseph. *Experiments and Observations on Different Kinds of Air.* Birmingham, 1774-1777. Quoted in: Hall, Thomas S. A Source Book in Animal Biology. New York: McGraw-Hill Book Co., Inc., 1951.

7. Swammerdam, Jan. *The Book of Nature or, the History of Insects.* Translated by Thomas Flloyd, revised and improved by John Hill, M.D. London: C. G. Seyffert, 1758.

8. Galvani, Luigi. *De Viribus Electricitatis in Motu Musculari Commentarius.* Mutinae, 1791. Reprinted by permission of the publishers from: Magie, William Francis. A Source Book in Physics. Cambridge, Mass.: Copyright 1935, 1963, by the President and Fellows of Harvard College.

9. Galvani, Luigi. *De Viribus Electricitatis in Motu Musculari Commentarius.* Mutinae, 1791. Quoted in: Darrow, Floyd L. The New World of Physical Discovery. Indianapolis: The Bobbs-Merrill Co., 1930. By permission of the Bobbs-Merrill Co.

10. Volta, Alessandro. *Collezione del Opere.* Firenze, 1816. Quoted in: Hall, R. A. The Scientific Revolution. New York: Longman's, Green & Co., 1954.

11. von Helmholtz, Hermann. "Messungen ueber Fortpflanzungsgeschwindigkeit der Reizung in den Nerven," in *Archiv fur Anatomie, Physiologie, und Wissenschaftliche Medizin,* 1852. Translated by M. and V. Hamburger and T. S. Hall, and quoted in: Hall, Thomas S. A Source Book in Animal Biology. New York: McGraw-Hill Book Co., Inc., 1951.

12. Ecker, Alexander. *The Anatomy of the Frog.* Translated, with annotations and additions, by George Haslam. Oxford: The Clarendon Press, 1889. By permission of the Clarendon Press.

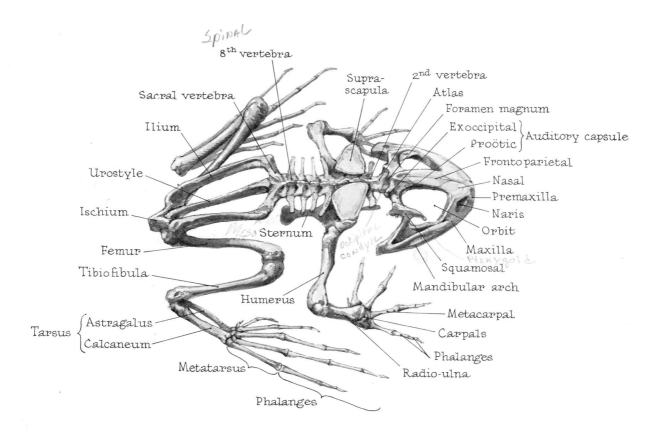

Spinal

8th vertebra

Supra-
scapula

2nd vertebra

Atlas

Foramen magnum

Exoccipital
Proötic } Auditory capsule

Frontoparietal

Nasal

Premaxilla

Naris

Orbit

Maxilla

Squamosal

Mandibular arch

Sacral vertebra

Ilium

Urostyle

Ischium

Meso Sternum

Femur

Tibiofibula

Humerus

occipital
condyle

Pterygoid

Metacarpal

Carpals

Phalanges

Radio-ulna

Tarsus { Astragalus
Calcaneum

Metatarsus

Phalanges

DORSOLATERAL VIEW OF THE SKELETON

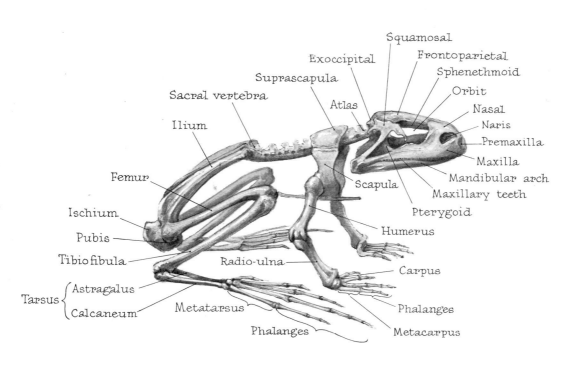

Squamosal

Exoccipital

Frontoparietal

Suprascapula

Sphenethmoid

Sacral vertebra

Atlas

Orbit

Ilium

Nasal

Naris

Premaxilla

Maxilla

Mandibular arch

Maxillary teeth

Femur

Scapula

Ischium

Pterygoid

Pubis

Humerus

Tibiofibula

Radio-ulna

Carpus

Tarsus { Astragalus
Calcaneum

Metatarsus

Phalanges

Phalanges

Metacarpus

LATERAL VIEW OF THE SKELETON

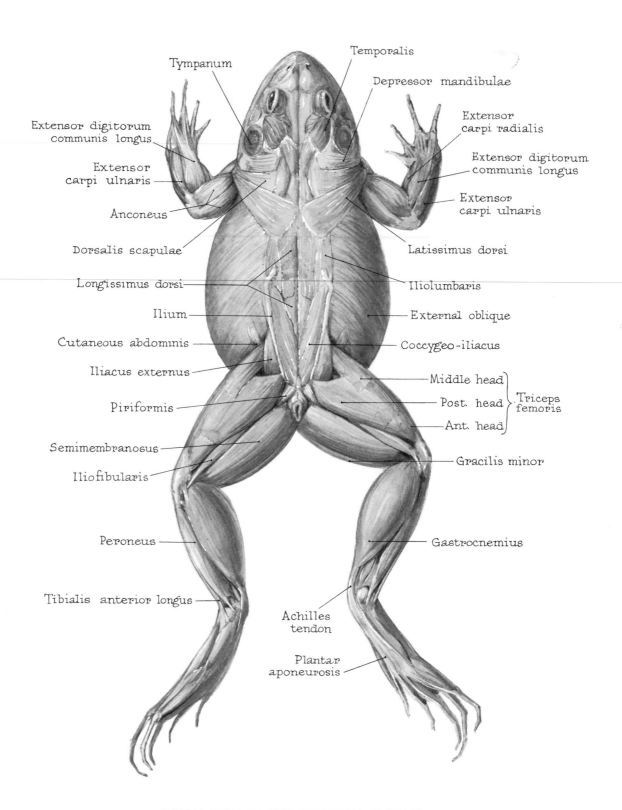

Tympanum

Temporalis

Depressor mandibulae

Extensor digitorum communis longus

Extensor carpi ulnaris

Anconeus

Dorsalis scapulae

Longissimus dorsi

Ilium

Cutaneous abdominis

Iliacus externus

Piriformis

Semimembranosus

Iliofibularis

Peroneus

Tibialis anterior longus

Extensor carpi radialis

Extensor digitorum communis longus

Extensor carpi ulnaris

Latissimus dorsi

Iliolumbaris

External oblique

Coccygeo-iliacus

Middle head

Post. head — Triceps femoris

Ant. head

Gracilis minor

Gastrocnemius

Achilles tendon

Plantar aponeurosis

DORSAL VIEW OF THE SUPERFICIAL MUSCLES

16

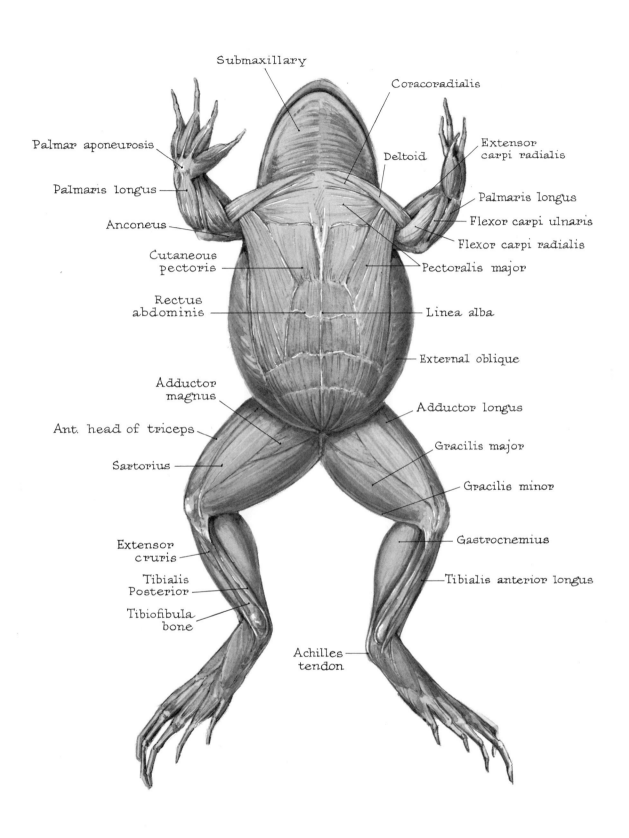

Submaxillary

Coracoradialis

Palmar aponeurosis

Extensor
carpi radialis

Deltoid

Palmaris longus

Palmaris longus

Flexor carpi ulnaris

Anconeus

Flexor carpi radialis

Cutaneous
pectoris

Pectoralis major

Rectus
abdominis

Linea alba

External oblique

Adductor
magnus

Adductor longus

Ant. head of triceps

Gracilis major

Sartorius

Gracilis minor

Extensor
cruris

Gastrocnemius

Tibialis
Posterior

Tibialis anterior longus

Tibiofibula
bone

Achilles
tendon

VENTRAL VIEW OF THE SUPERFICIAL MUSCLES

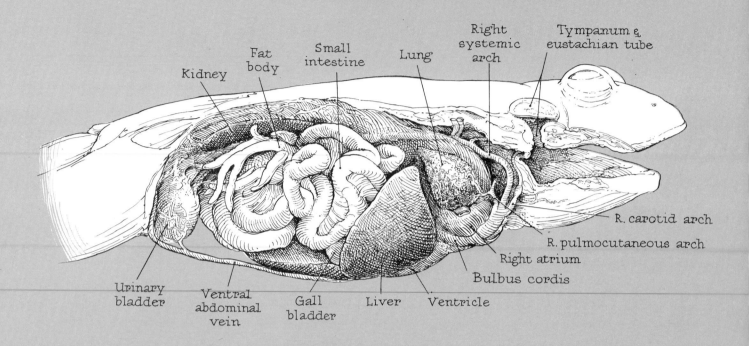

Kidney · Fat body · Small intestine · Lung · Right systemic arch · Tympanum & eustachian tube

R. carotid arch

R. pulmocutaneous arch

Right atrium

Bulbus cordis

Urinary bladder · Ventral abdominal vein · Gall bladder · Liver · Ventricle

**VISCERA IN A MALE SPECIMEN,
RIGHT LATERAL VIEW**

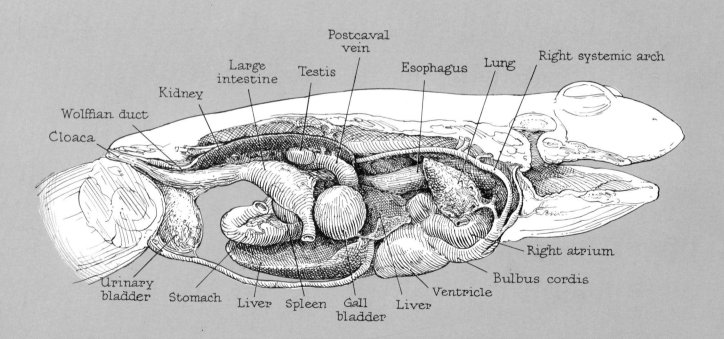

Postcaval vein

Large intestine · Testis · Esophagus · Lung · Right systemic arch

Kidney

Wolffian duct

Cloaca

Right atrium

Bulbus cordis

Urinary bladder · Stomach · Liver · Spleen · Gall bladder · Liver · Ventricle

The small intestine, right fat body, and right
lobe of the liver are removed.

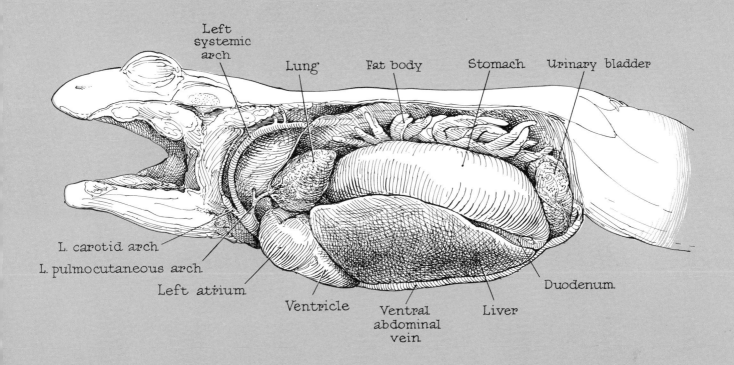

Left
systemic
arch

Lung

Fat body

Stomach

Urinary bladder

L. carotid arch

L. pulmocutaneous arch

Left atrium

Ventricle

Ventral
abdominal
vein

Liver

Duodenum

VISCERA IN A MALE SPECIMEN,
LEFT LATERAL VIEW

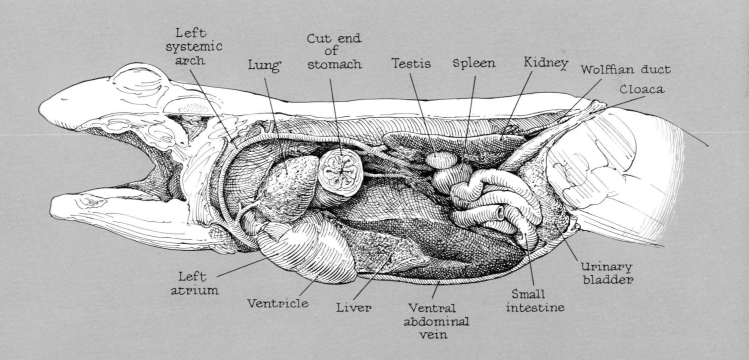

Left
systemic
arch

Lung

Cut end
of
stomach

Testis

Spleen

Kidney

Wolffian duct

Cloaca

Left
atrium

Ventricle

Liver

Ventral
abdominal
vein

Small
intestine

Urinary
bladder

The stomach, duodenum, left fat body, and
anterior part of the left hepatic lobe are removed.

19

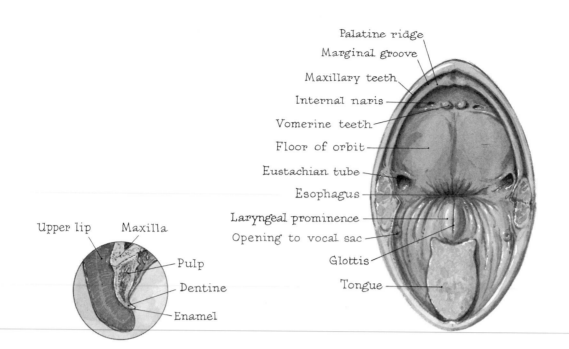

Palatine ridge
Marginal groove
Maxillary teeth
Internal naris
Vomerine teeth
Floor of orbit
Eustachian tube
Esophagus
Laryngeal prominence
Opening to vocal sac
Glottis
Tongue

Upper lip
Maxilla
Pulp
Dentine
Enamel

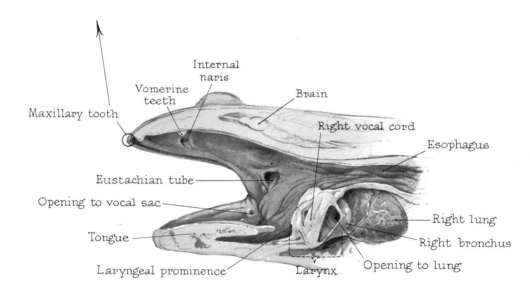

Maxillary tooth
Vomerine teeth
Internal naris
Brain
Right vocal cord
Esophagus
Eustachian tube
Opening to vocal sac
Tongue
Laryngeal prominence
Larynx
Opening to lung
Right lung
Right bronchus

THE MOUTH AND LUNGS

The larynx is a musculocartilaginous structure containing the vocal cords. The frog's call is produced when the vocal cords are set into vibration by air driven back and forth between the mouth and the lungs. The call may be varied by the laryngeal muscles, which alter the tension on the vocal cords. Because the mouth and nares are kept tightly closed when the call is produced, the frog is able to call under water. The sound is reinforced by the vocal sacs (present in males only), which expand and act as resonators. They are located under the submaxillary muscle and open into the floor of the mouth. Although frogs call at times other than the mating season, attracting mates is apparently the chief function of the voice. It is only the males who call loudly, the females being either mute or having voices softer than those of the males.

RESPIRATION

In frogs the exchange of carbon dioxide and oxygen between blood and air occurs at three different sites: the skin (cutaneous respiration), the lungs (pulmonary respiration), and the mucous membrane of the mouth and pharynx (buccopharyngeal respiration). In these places blood flows in capillaries separated from the air only by a thin, moist membrane, the condition necessary for aeration of the blood. The importance of these three kinds of respiration varies in different amphibians. Some salamanders have no lungs, depending wholly on buccopharyngeal and cutaneous respiration, while others have both lungs and external gills.

Mucous glands in the skin, large subcutaneous lymph spaces, and a semi-aquatic life keep the frog's skin moist and make cutaneous respiration possible in air as well as in water. Prolonged exposure to a warm, dry atmosphere will cause the skin to dry out, making cutaneous respiration impossible and eventually killing the frog. During hibernation when the temperature is low and the metabolic rate is reduced, the frog does not breathe with its lungs, but depends mainly on cutaneous respiration. Under normal conditions of temperature and activity, however, a frog can live only a few days without employing pulmonary respiration. The relative roles of the three modes of respiration are not fully understood, but experiments have shown that more carbon dioxide is given off through the skin than through the lungs, and that more oxygen is taken in through the lungs than through the skin.

Pulmonary and cutaneous respiration are of approximately equal importance and account for the majority of the exchange of oxygen and carbon dioxide. Buccopharyngeal respiration accounts for only a small part of the respiratory exchange, and the regular oscillatory movements of the floor of the mouth are thought to be primarily involved in olfaction rather than in respiration.

Reptiles, birds, and mammals draw in air by expanding the cavity containing the lungs, but the frog lacks movable ribs and must force air into the lungs with its mouth. When a frog is at rest, the floor of the mouth may be seen to make regular oscillatory movements. At irregular intervals these movements are interrupted by a sudden contraction and expansion of the body wall, after which the oscillatory movements are resumed. These observations may be explained by dividing the respiratory cycle into three phases as follows:

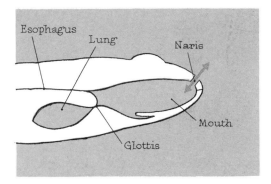

Buccopharyngeal respiration: The floor of the mouth undergoes regular oscillatory movements which force air in and out through the nares. The lungs are full of air and the glottis is closed.

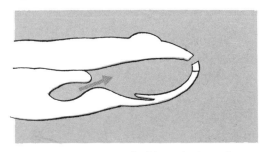

Expiration: Air is expelled from the lungs by contraction of the abdominal muscles aided by the natural elasticity of the lungs.

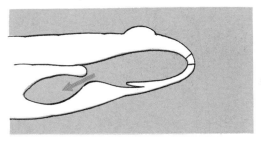

Inspiration: The abdominal muscles relax, the nares close, and the floor of the mouth is raised, driving the air back into the lungs. During strong inspiration the eyes may be drawn inward, which further increases the pressure within the mouth by causing a bulge in the floor of the orbit. The glottis is then closed, the nares open, and buccopharyngeal respiration and olfaction are resumed.

This account of the respiratory mechanism (based on Gaupp and Holmes) is the one given by most textbooks. An account of the experiments supporting this interpretation is given by Martin (1878). Cherian (1956) reports a different respiratory cycle observed in *Rana hexadactyla* and includes a discussion of recent publications on the subject.

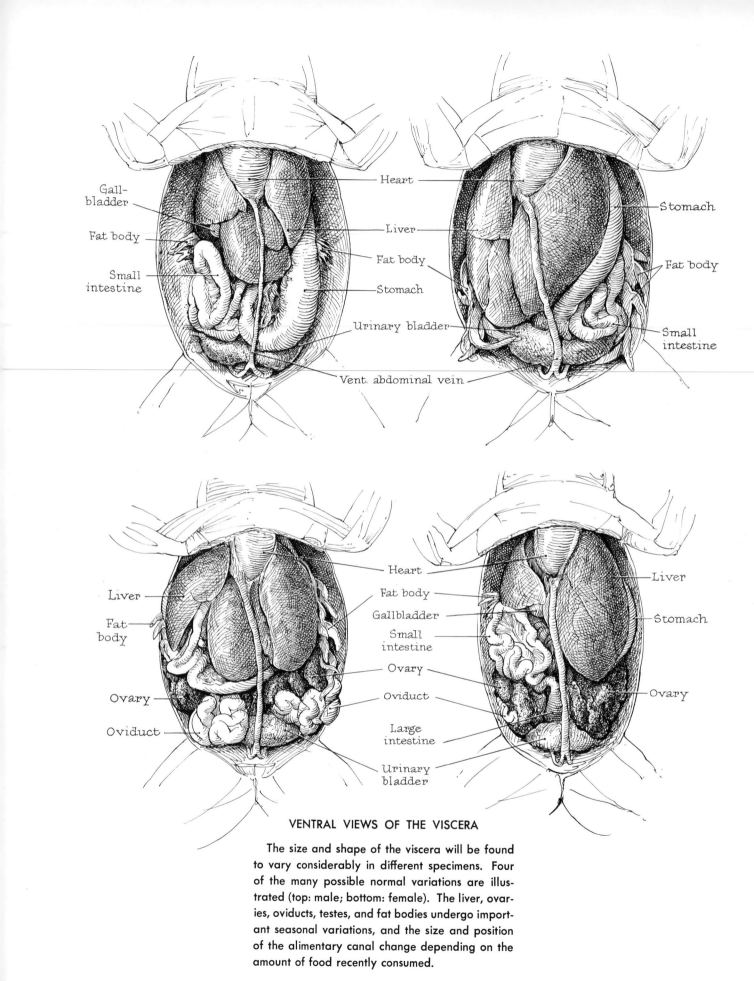

Gallbladder

Fat body

Small intestine

Heart

Liver

Fat body

Stomach

Urinary bladder

Vent. abdominal vein

Stomach

Fat body

Small intestine

Liver

Fat body

Ovary

Oviduct

Heart

Fat body

Gallbladder

Small intestine

Ovary

Oviduct

Large intestine

Urinary bladder

Liver

Stomach

Ovary

VENTRAL VIEWS OF THE VISCERA

The size and shape of the viscera will be found to vary considerably in different specimens. Four of the many possible normal variations are illustrated (top: male; bottom: female). The liver, ovaries, oviducts, testes, and fat bodies undergo important seasonal variations, and the size and position of the alimentary canal change depending on the amount of food recently consumed.

THE ALIMENTARY CANAL AND ASSOCIATED ORGANS

Tadpoles eat a mixed diet of vegetable and animal food, but the adult frog is carnivorous, eating a variety of living prey such as insects, snails, worms, spiders, and even smaller frogs. A hungry frog will snap at any small moving object, but ignores a motionless prey.

The frog's tongue is a very mobile organ which serves a vital function in obtaining food. It is attached at the front of the jaw. To catch an insect, the frog flips out his tongue, extends it, and curls it around the insect, which adheres to the sticky surface and is pulled back into the mouth (see page 27).

Frogs do not drink, but absorb all the water they need through the skin by osmosis, a function connected with the large subcutaneous lymph spaces, the thin skin, and the loose attachment of the skin to the body.

The esophagus and stomach are capable of great distention, enabling the frog to swallow relatively large prey. The stomach serves as a place of storage where food is acted on chemically and physically before being passed on to the small intestine, where absorption of food materials into the blood and lymph takes place. Much of the epithelium of the mouth and esophagus is provided with cilia which supplement the action of peristalsis. The walls of the esophagus, the small intestine, and the large intestine are provided with an outer layer of longitudinal muscle and an inner layer of circular muscle which force the food along by peristaltic contractions. In the stomach the longitudinal layer is mostly absent, but the circular layer is very thick and serves the additional function of breaking up the food, which is only partially crushed by the rudimentary teeth. The mucous membrane forming the inner lining of the alimentary canal secretes digestive juices and mucus, and its surface forms many folds which increase the absorptive area. Food materials which have been acted on by the digestive juices are absorbed through the epithelium of the small intestine into the capillaries and lymphatics to be carried to their destinations.

Frogs do not have the stores of subcutaneous fatty tissue found in birds and mammals, but small fat deposits have been found at various sites in well-nourished frogs before hibernation. The fat stored in the fat bodies is a reserve supply of nutriment most of which is used during breeding, but this supply may be used for the whole body in an emergency. Much of the nutriment which enables the frog to survive hibernation is stored in the liver, and for this reason the size of the liver will be found to vary considerably in different specimens, depending on the time of year when they were collected. In the fall before hibernation, the liver may be two or three times as large as it is in the spring. The hibernating frog also draws on nutriment stored in the muscles, which decrease in weight in relation to the rest of the body during winter. Because of their low metabolic rate and their ability to live on their own tissues, amphibians are able to live for long periods without food. Both frogs and salamanders have survived fasts of over a year.

Although it is connected with the alimentary canal, the liver is not primarily an organ of digestion. In addition to the elaboration and storage of fats and glycogen, the liver has many other functions, including the formation of urea (a waste product of protein metabolism), the destruction of red blood corpuscles, and the secretion of bile, which is stored in the gall bladder and enters the alimentary canal via the bile duct. Bile contains no digestive enzymes. Some of its constituents are waste products, but it also contains salts which are functional in the breakdown and absorption of fats. The pancreas secretes digestive enzymes which break down food into substances which can be absorbed through the intestinal epithelium. It also secretes a hormone—insulin—which regulates the amount of sugar in the blood. The enzymes enter the small intestine via the bile duct, which connects with the pancreatic ducts within the substance of the pancreas, while insulin is secreted directly into the blood stream. The spleen functions in the formation, storage, and destruction of blood corpuscles, and also contains cells which take up pigment and other foreign matter in the blood.

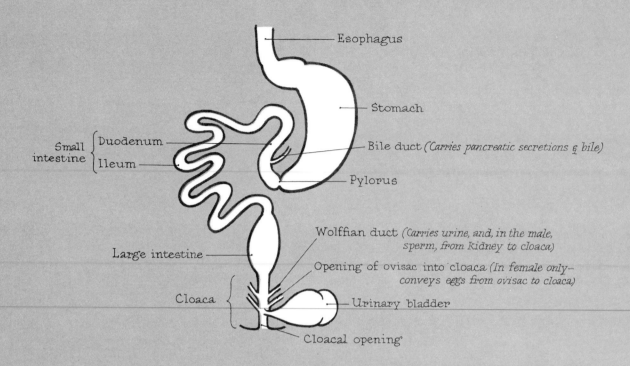

Esophagus

Stomach

Small intestine { Duodenum
Ileum

Bile duct *(Carries pancreatic secretions & bile)*

Pylorus

Wolffian duct *(Carries urine, and, in the male, sperm, from kidney to cloaca)*

Large intestine

Opening of ovisac into cloaca *(In female only— conveys eggs from ovisac to cloaca)*

Cloaca {

Urinary bladder

Cloacal opening

THE ALIMENTARY CANAL

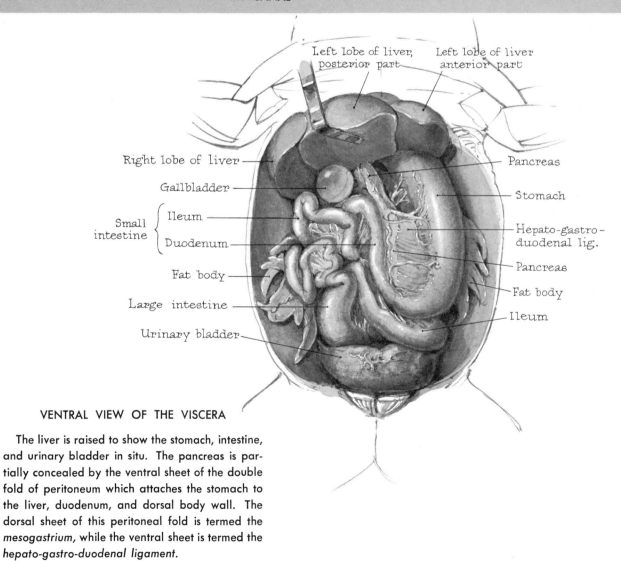

Left lobe of liver, posterior part

Left lobe of liver anterior part

Right lobe of liver

Pancreas

Gallbladder

Stomach

Small intestine { Ileum
Duodenum

Hepato-gastro-duodenal lig.

Pancreas

Fat body

Fat body

Large intestine

Ileum

Urinary bladder

VENTRAL VIEW OF THE VISCERA

The liver is raised to show the stomach, intestine, and urinary bladder in situ. The pancreas is partially concealed by the ventral sheet of the double fold of peritoneum which attaches the stomach to the liver, duodenum, and dorsal body wall. The dorsal sheet of this peritoneal fold is termed the *mesogastrium,* while the ventral sheet is termed the *hepato-gastro-duodenal ligament.*

24

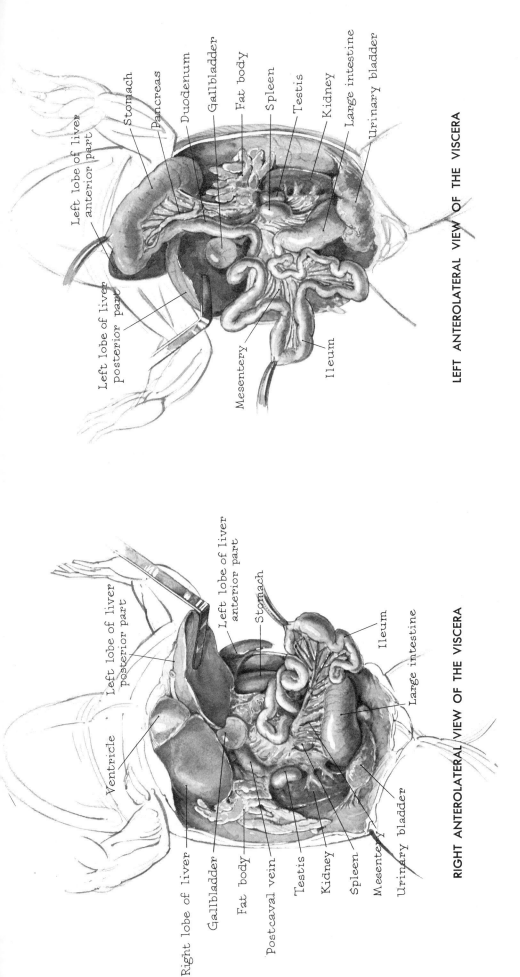

Left lobe of liver anterior part
Stomach
Pancreas
Duodenum
Gallbladder
Fat body
Spleen
Testis
Kidney
Large intestine
Urinary bladder

Left lobe of liver posterior part

Mesentery

Ileum

LEFT ANTEROLATERAL VIEW OF THE VISCERA

Left lobe of liver posterior part
Left lobe of liver anterior part
Stomach

Ventricle

Ileum

Large intestine

Right lobe of liver
Gallbladder
Fat body
Postcaval vein
Testis
Kidney
Spleen
Mesentery
Urinary bladder

RIGHT ANTEROLATERAL VIEW OF THE VISCERA

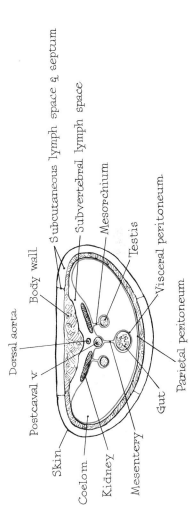

Subcutaneous lymph space & septum
Subvertebral lymph space
Mesorchium
Testis
Visceral peritoneum

Body wall

Dorsal aorta

Postcaval v.

Skin

Coelom
Kidney
Mesentery
Gut
Parietal peritoneum

CROSS-SECTION OF THE ABDOMEN

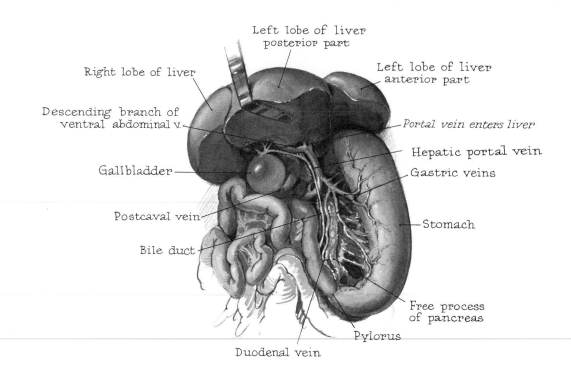

Right lobe of liver

Left lobe of liver
posterior part

Left lobe of liver
anterior part

Descending branch of
ventral abdominal v.

Portal vein enters liver

Hepatic portal vein

Gallbladder

Gastric veins

Postcaval vein

Stomach

Bile duct

Free process
of pancreas

Duodenal vein

Pylorus

VENTRAL VIEW OF THE STOMACH AND LIVER

Most of the hepato-gastro-duodenal ligament and the pancreas are removed, exposing those portions of the bile duct and the hepatic portal vein which lie within the pancreas. Pancreatic ducts connect with the bile duct within the substance of the pancreas, but they are too small to dissect by ordinary methods. The arteries are omitted.

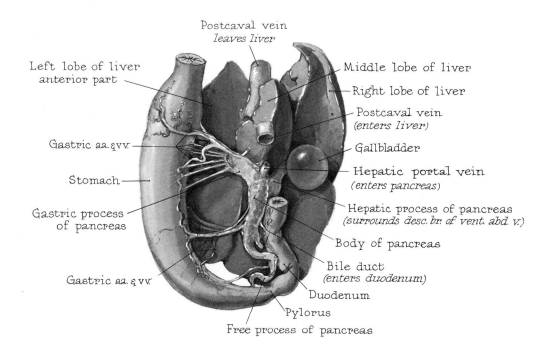

Postcaval vein
leaves liver

Left lobe of liver
anterior part

Middle lobe of liver

Right lobe of liver

Postcaval vein
(enters liver)

Gastric aa. & vv.

Gallbladder

Stomach

Hepatic portal vein
(enters pancreas)

Gastric process
of pancreas

Hepatic process of pancreas
(surrounds desc. br. of vent. abd. v.)

Body of pancreas

Bile duct
(enters duodenum)

Gastric aa. & vv.

Duodenum

Pylorus

Free process of pancreas

DORSAL VIEW OF THE STOMACH AND LIVER

The mesogastrium and the hepato-gastro-duodenal ligament are removed. The pancreas is intact and conceals those portions of the hepatic portal vein and the bile duct which lie within it.

A BULLFROG SEIZES ITS PREY

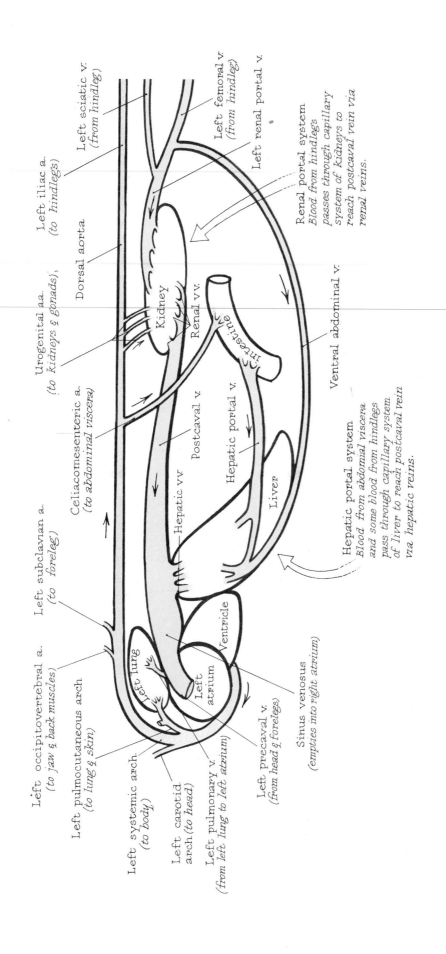

Left occipitovertebral a.
(to jaw & back muscles)

Left subclavian a.
(to foreleg)

Left pulmocutaneous arch
(to lung & skin)

Left systemic arch
(to body)

Left carotid
arch (to head)

Left pulmonary v.
(from left lung to left atrium)

Left precaval v.
(from head & forelegs)

Sinus venosus
(empties into right atrium)

Left occipitovertebral a.

Left lung

Ventricle

Left atrium

Left sciatic v.
(from hindleg)

Left iliac a.
(to hindlegs)

Left femoral v.
(from hindleg)

Left renal portal v.

Dorsal aorta

Urogenital aa.
(to kidneys & gonads)

Celiacomesenteric a.
(to abdominal viscera)

Kidney

Renal vv.

Intestine

Postcaval v.

Hepatic vv.

Hepatic portal v.

Liver

Ventral abdominal v.

Renal portal system
Blood from hindlegs
passes through capillary
system of kidneys to
reach postcaval vein via
renal veins.

Hepatic portal system
Blood from abdominal viscera
and some blood from hindlegs
pass through capillary system
of liver to reach postcaval vein
via hepatic veins.

LATERAL VIEW OF THE
CIRCULATORY SYSTEM (schematic)

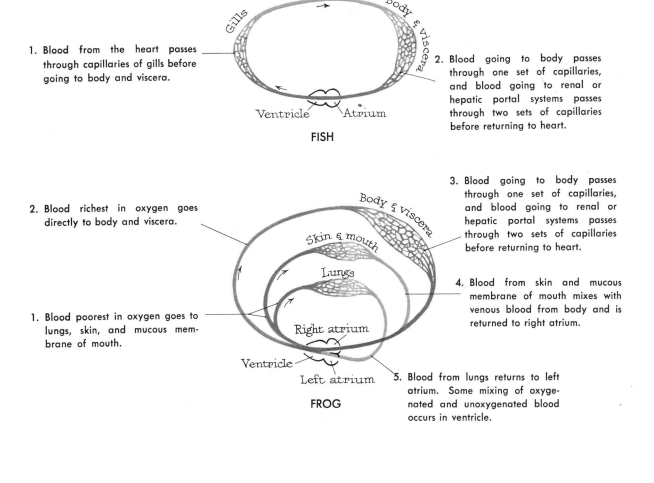

1. Blood from the heart passes through capillaries of gills before going to body and viscera.

2. Blood going to body passes through one set of capillaries, and blood going to renal or hepatic portal systems passes through two sets of capillaries before returning to heart.

FISH

2. Blood richest in oxygen goes directly to body and viscera.

1. Blood poorest in oxygen goes to lungs, skin, and mucous membrane of mouth.

3. Blood going to body passes through one set of capillaries, and blood going to renal or hepatic portal systems passes through two sets of capillaries before returning to heart.

4. Blood from skin and mucous membrane of mouth mixes with venous blood from body and is returned to right atrium.

5. Blood from lungs returns to left atrium. Some mixing of oxygenated and unoxygenated blood occurs in ventricle.

FROG

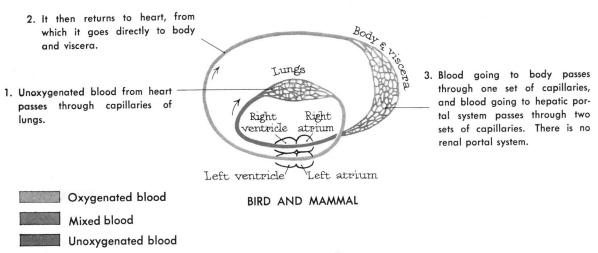

2. It then returns to heart, from which it goes directly to body and viscera.

1. Unoxygenated blood from heart passes through capillaries of lungs.

3. Blood going to body passes through one set of capillaries, and blood going to hepatic portal system passes through two sets of capillaries. There is no renal portal system.

☐ Oxygenated blood

☐ Mixed blood

☐ Unoxygenated blood

BIRD AND MAMMAL

DIAGRAMS OF VERTEBRATE CIRCULATORY SYSTEMS

Because of their greater activity, terrestrial animals require a more efficient circulatory system than do fish. This has been achieved by a reduction in the number of capillary nets through which the blood passes before returning to the heart and also by the development of a double circuit in the heart to pump oxygenated blood directly to the body and viscera. The frog is descended from a vertebrate ancestor representing an intermediate stage in this development.

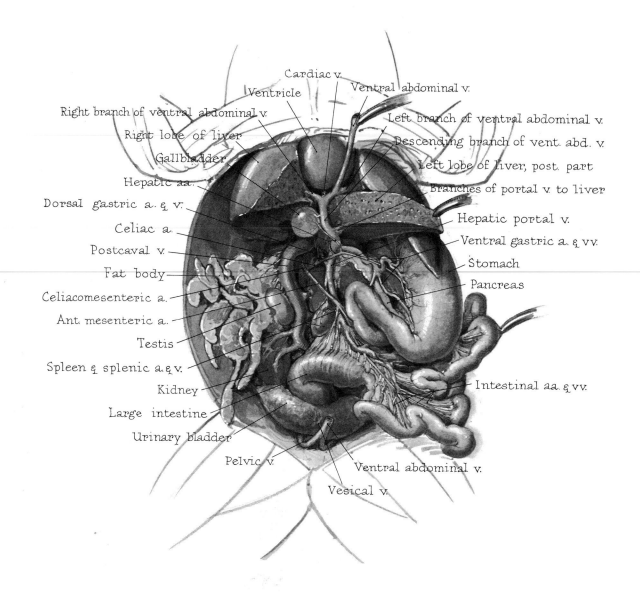

Cardiac v.
Ventricle
Ventral abdominal v.
Right branch of ventral abdominal v.
Left branch of ventral abdominal v.
Right lobe of liver
Descending branch of vent. abd. v.
Gallbladder
Left lobe of liver, post. part
Hepatic aa.
Branches of portal v. to liver
Dorsal gastric a. & v.
Hepatic portal v.
Celiac a.
Ventral gastric a. & vv.
Postcaval v.
Stomach
Fat body
Pancreas
Celiacomesenteric a.
Ant. mesenteric a.
Testis
Spleen & splenic a. & v.
Intestinal aa. & vv.
Kidney
Large intestine
Urinary bladder
Pelvic v.
Ventral abdominal v.
Vesical v.

THE HEPATIC PORTAL SYSTEM

The bile duct, much of the pancreas, and part
of the liver are removed to show the course of the
hepatic portal vein. The celiacomesenteric artery
carries blood to the intestinal capillaries where the
products of digestion are absorbed. The blood
returns to the liver via the hepatic portal vein.
Within the liver the blood again passes through a
system of capillaries where many of the nutritive
elements are picked up to be transformed and
stored by the hepatic cells. The blood then returns
to the postcaval vein via the hepatic veins.

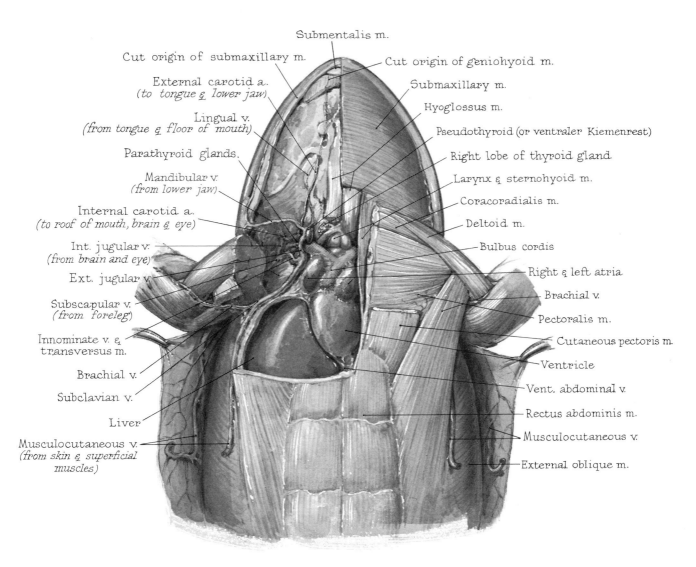

Submentalis m.

Cut origin of submaxillary m.

External carotid a.
(to tongue & lower jaw)

Lingual v.
(from tongue & floor of mouth)

Parathyroid glands.

Mandibular v.
(from lower jaw)

Internal carotid a.
(to roof of mouth, brain & eye)

Int. jugular v.
(from brain and eye)

Ext. jugular v.

Subscapular v.
(from foreleg)

Innominate v. &
transversus m.

Brachial v.

Subclavian v.

Liver

Musculocutaneous v.
(from skin & superficial
muscles)

Cut origin of geniohyoid m.

Submaxillary m.

Hyoglossus m.

Pseudothyroid (or ventraler Kiemenrest)

Right lobe of thyroid gland.

Larynx & sternohyoid m.

Coracoradialis m.

Deltoid m.

Bulbus cordis

Right & left atria

Brachial v.

Pectoralis m.

Cutaneous pectoris m.

Ventricle

Vent. abdominal v.

Rectus abdominis m.

Musculocutaneous v.

External oblique m.

THE HEART AND SUPERFICIAL VEINS

On the left the muscles are intact. On the right the shoulder girdle is cut to show the superficial branches of the veins anterior to the heart. The geniohyoid and hyoglossus muscles are cut to reveal the right lobe of the thyroid gland. In amphibians the thyroid gland consists of two separate lobes which lie on either side of the larynx. They are composed of tiny masses of rounded follicles and are difficult to distinguish from the surrounding tissue. The thyroid secretion is of importance in the control of metamorphosis, growth, and metabolism. The parathyroid glands, which function in the regulation of normal calcium and phosphate levels in the blood, consist of two pairs of small rounded bodies. One pair lies lateral to each external jugular vein. The pseudothyroid (or *ventraler Kiemenrest*), which is sometimes confused with the thyroid or with the parathyroids, is a lymphoid body of unknown function. It is easily seen grossly, while identification of the thyroid and parathyroids usually requires the use of a lens or

dissecting microscope.

The heart is enclosed within a membranous sac, the pericardium, which separates it from the coelom. The pericardium is intact in this view but is removed in the following views.

Oxygenated blood from the mucous membrane of the mouth returns via the internal jugular vein and the musculocutaneous vein. The musculocutaneous vein also carries oxygenated blood from the skin, along with a small amount of unoxygenated blood from the superficial muscles. Cutaneous respiration is facilitated by the rich network of blood vessels supplying the skin.

The anterior portion of the transversus muscles inserts on the esophagus, larynx, hyoid, and pericardium, forming a dome around the lungs. According to Gaupp, contraction of this muscle forces air out of the lungs during expiration, and its attachment on the esophagus enables the frog to voluntarily open the esophagus wide when swallowing large prey.

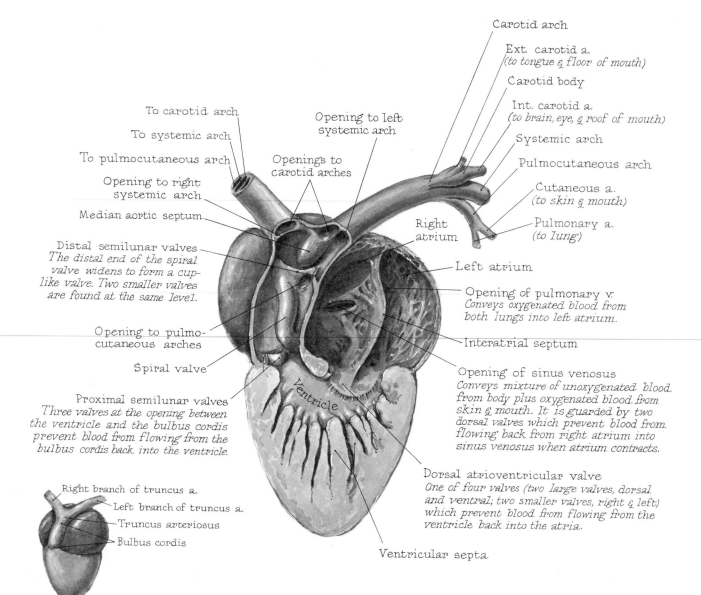

Carotid arch

Ext. carotid a.
(to tongue & floor of mouth)

Carotid body

Int. carotid a.
(to brain, eye, & roof of mouth)

Systemic arch

Pulmocutaneous arch

Cutaneous a.
(to skin & mouth)

Pulmonary a.
(to lung)

To carotid arch

To systemic arch

To pulmocutaneous arch

Opening to right
systemic arch

Median aortic septum

Distal semilunar valves
*The distal end of the spiral
valve widens to form a cup-
like valve. Two smaller valves
are found at the same level.*

Opening to pulmo-
cutaneous arches

Spiral valve

Proximal semilunar valves
*Three valves at the opening between
the ventricle and the bulbus cordis
prevent blood from flowing from the
bulbus cordis back into the ventricle.*

Opening to left
systemic arch

Openings to
carotid arches

Right
atrium

Left atrium

Opening of pulmonary v.
*Conveys oxygenated blood from
both lungs into left atrium.*

Interatrial septum

Opening of sinus venosus
*Conveys mixture of unoxygenated blood
from body plus oxygenated blood from
skin & mouth. It is guarded by two
dorsal valves which prevent blood from
flowing back from right atrium into
sinus venosus when atrium contracts.*

Dorsal atrioventricular valve
*One of four valves (two large valves, dorsal
and ventral; two smaller valves, right & left)
which prevent blood from flowing from the
ventricle back into the atria.*

Ventricle

Ventricular septa

Right branch of truncus a.

Left branch of truncus a.

Truncus arteriosus

Bulbus cordis

VENTRAL VIEW OF THE HEART

The ventral sides of the atria, the ventricle, and the *bulbus cordis* and *truncus arteriosus* are removed to reveal the interior of the heart. The right atrium, which is larger than the left, extends behind the *bulbus cordis* and its intact ventral wall is seen to the right of the *bulbus cordis*.

The spiral valve is attached to the dorsal wall of the *bulbus cordis,* but its ventral border is unattached. When the *bulbus cordis* is relaxed, blood is free to flow on either side of the spiral valve.

When the *bulbus cordis* contracts during the second phase of systole, the ventral border of the spiral valve is pressed against the ventral wall of the *bulbus cordis,* closing off the left side of the *bulbus cordis* and preventing oxygenated blood from entering the pulmocutaneous arches. Blood still flows freely to the right of the spiral valve, however. This mechanism explains the significance of the position of the opening to the pulmocutaneous arches.

CIRCULATION IN THE HEART OF THE FROG

Two kinds of blood enter the heart. Relatively unoxygenated blood (consisting of unoxygenated blood from the body mixed with oxygenated blood from the skin and mouth) enters the right atrium. Blood of somewhat higher oxygen content returns from the lungs to the left atrium. It is generally agreed that there is partial separation of these two kinds of blood within the ventricle and the *bulbus cordis* with the result that the lungs receive blood of low oxygen content and the body receives blood of higher oxygen content.

Early investigators thought that oxygenated and unoxygenated blood mixed completely in the ventricle. In 1835, by cutting off the tip of the ventricle Mayer observed that two streams emerged—a light (oxygenated) and a dark (unoxygenated)—which showed that the mixture was not complete. Circulation in the frog heart was further studied by Bruecke in 1851 and Sabatier in 1873, who attempted to explain the mechanisms by which the separation of the blood streams is effected. Gaupp reported the work of Sabatier in his revision of Ecker's *Anatomie des Frosches.* Sabatier's interpretation, known as the "classical hypothesis," has been followed by many textbooks and it is his interpretation on which the following account is based.

First phase of systole: When the ventricle contracts, the first blood to enter the *bulbus cordis* is relatively unoxygenated. It goes mainly to the pulmocutaneous arches because the pressure in these arches is lower than the pressure in the systemic and carotid arches. During this phase, blood flow to the systemic and carotid arches is also inhibited by the *valvula paradoxa,* a small valve at the outer end of the systemic arch, and by the contraction of the carotid body. Structural features of significance in this phase are the division of the ventricle into deep septa which act as baffles to prevent the two blood streams from mixing, and the position of the opening to the *bulbus cordis,* closer to the source of the less oxygenated blood which enters it first.

Second phase of systole: Next follows blood of higher oxygen content. The *bulbus cordis* contracts and the spiral valve closes the passage to the pulmocutaneous arches, so that this mixed blood goes mainly to the systemic arches.

Continuation of second phase: Finally comes blood of highest oxygen content, and at this time the carotid bodies (which have up to now been in a state of contraction) open, allowing the most highly oxygenated blood to go to the head and brain. Simultaneously, further contraction of the *bulbus cordis* forces the median aortic septum to close the entrance to the left systemic arch, with the result that the body and kidneys (supplied mainly by the right systemic arch via the dorsal aorta and its branches) receive blood more highly oxygenated than that which goes to the abdominal viscera (supplied mainly by the left systemic arch via the celiacomesenteric artery).

Sabatier based his theory on observations of the living heart under direct illumination and on deductions from anatomical structure. Since Sabatier's time, numerous papers have been published on the problem of circulation in the frog heart and a number of techniques not available to Sabatier have been employed. None of the subsequent work has confirmed all of Sabatier's conclusions. His accounts of the function of the carotid body* and the *valvula paradoxa,* and his belief that the blood enters the three arches at different times have not been supported by recent work. It has also been shown that in many species the pressure of the blood in the pulmocutaneous arches is not significantly lower than it is in the carotid and systemic arches.

The extent of the separation of the two bloodstreams and the mechanisms by which the separation is accomplished are still the subject of controversy. Students interested in this question will find further information in Chapter Three of Moore's *Physiology of the Amphibia.*

---

* The functions of the carotid body are still not fully understood. It is thought to have a mechanical function in equalizing blood flow between the external and internal carotid arteries, and to have functions connected with blood pressure and with the detection of the oxygen tension of the blood.

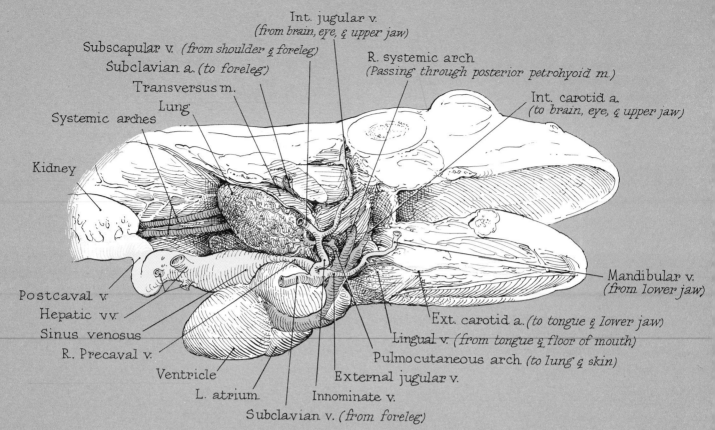

Int. jugular v.
(from brain, eye, & upper jaw)

Subscapular v. *(from shoulder & foreleg)*

Subclavian a. *(to foreleg)*

Transversus m.

Lung

Systemic arches

Kidney

R. systemic arch
(Passing through posterior petrohyoid m.)

Int. carotid a.
(to brain, eye, & upper jaw)

Mandibular v.
(from lower jaw)

Postcaval v.

Hepatic v.v.

Sinus venosus

R. Precaval v.

Ventricle

L. atrium

Innominate v.

Subclavian v. *(from foreleg)*

Ext. carotid a. *(to tongue & lower jaw)*

Lingual v. *(from tongue & floor of mouth)*

Pulmocutaneous arch *(to lung & skin)*

External jugular v.

RIGHT LATERAL VIEW OF THE HEART AND MAJOR VESSELS

The pectoral girdle is removed.

Pulmonary a. *(to lung)*
& cut end of cutaneous a. (to skin)

Occipitovertebral a.
(to jaw & back muscles)

Subclavian a. *(to foreleg)*

R. systemic arch

Eustachian tube

Int. carotid a.
(to brain, eye, & upper jaw)

Sinus venosus

R. precaval v.

R. atrium

Ventricle

Subclavian, Innominate, & Ext. jugular v.v.

L. atrium

Bulbus cordis

R. branch of truncus arteriosus

Pulmocutaneous arch

Carotid arch

Carotid body

Ext. carotid a. *(to tongue & lower jaw)*

Laryngeal a.

The veins are removed and the dissection is
carried deeper to show the occipitovertebral and

internal carotid arteries. The posterior petrohyoid
muscle is removed, revealing the right systemic
arch.

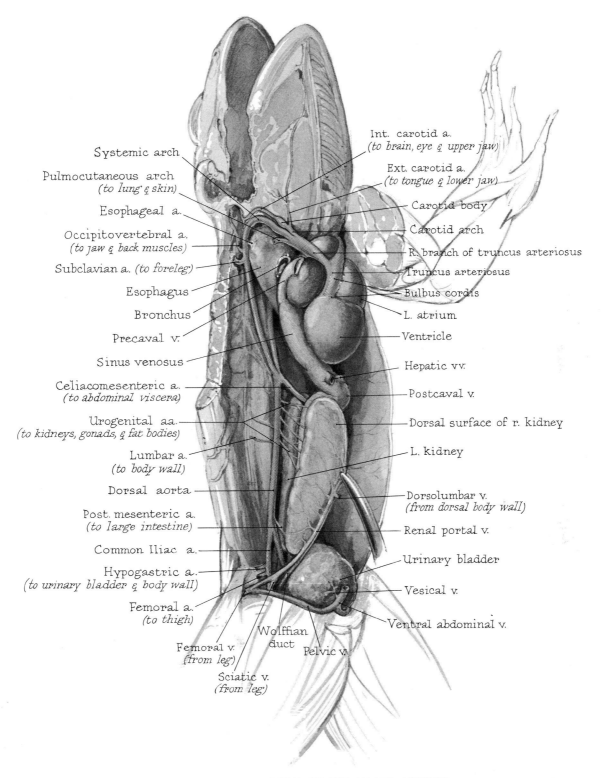

Int. carotid a.
(to brain, eye & upper jaw)

Ext. carotid a.
(to tongue & lower jaw)

Carotid body

Carotid arch

R. branch of truncus arteriosus

Truncus arteriosus

Bulbus cordis

L. atrium

Ventricle

Hepatic vv.

Postcaval v.

Dorsal surface of r. kidney

L. kidney

Dorsolumbar v.
(from dorsal body wall)

Renal portal v.

Urinary bladder

Vesical v.

Ventral abdominal v.

Systemic arch

Pulmocutaneous arch
(to lung & skin)

Esophageal a.

Occipitovertebral a.
(to jaw & back muscles)

Subclavian a. *(to foreleg)*

Esophagus

Bronchus

Precaval v.

Sinus venosus

Celiacomesenteric a.
(to abdominal viscera)

Urogenital aa.
(to kidneys, gonads, & fat bodies)

Lumbar a.
(to body wall)

Dorsal aorta

Post. mesenteric a.
(to large intestine)

Common Iliac a.

Hypogastric a.
(to urinary bladder & body wall)

Femoral a.
(to thigh)

Femoral v.
(from leg)

Wolffian duct

Pelvic v.

Sciatic v.
(from leg)

ANTEROLATERAL VIEW OF THE MAJOR ARTERIES

The stomach, intestine, right lung, right foreleg, and much of the body wall are removed. The right kidney is retracted ventrad to show its dorsal surface. The esophageal artery, which arises directly from the systemic arch in this specimen, often arises as a branch of the occipitovertebral artery. After giving off the femoral artery, the common iliac artery continues into the leg as the sciatic artery.

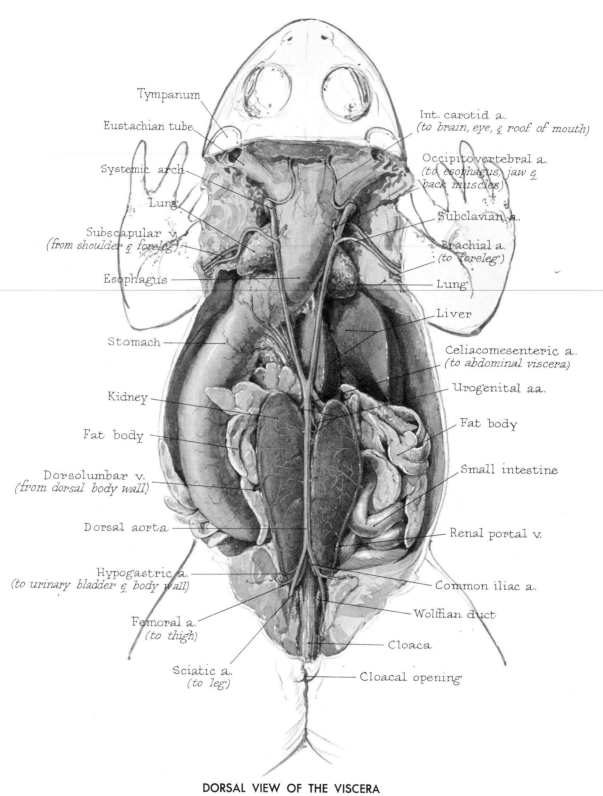

Tympanum

Eustachian tube

Systemic arch

Lung

Subscapular v.
(from shoulder & foreleg)

Esophagus

Stomach

Kidney

Fat body

Dorsolumbar v.
(from dorsal body wall)

Dorsal aorta

Hypogastric a.
(to urinary bladder & body wall)

Femoral a.
(to thigh)

Sciatic a.
(to leg)

Int. carotid a.
(to brain, eye, & roof of mouth)

Occipitovertebral a.
*(to esophagus, jaw &
back muscles)*

Subclavian a.

Brachial a.
(to foreleg)

Lung

Liver

Celiacomesenteric a.
(to abdominal viscera)

Urogenital aa.

Fat body

Small intestine

Renal portal v.

Common iliac a.

Wolffian duct

Cloaca

Cloacal opening

**DORSAL VIEW OF THE VISCERA
IN A MALE SPECIMEN**

The dorsal body wall and the spinal column are
removed to show the viscera in situ.

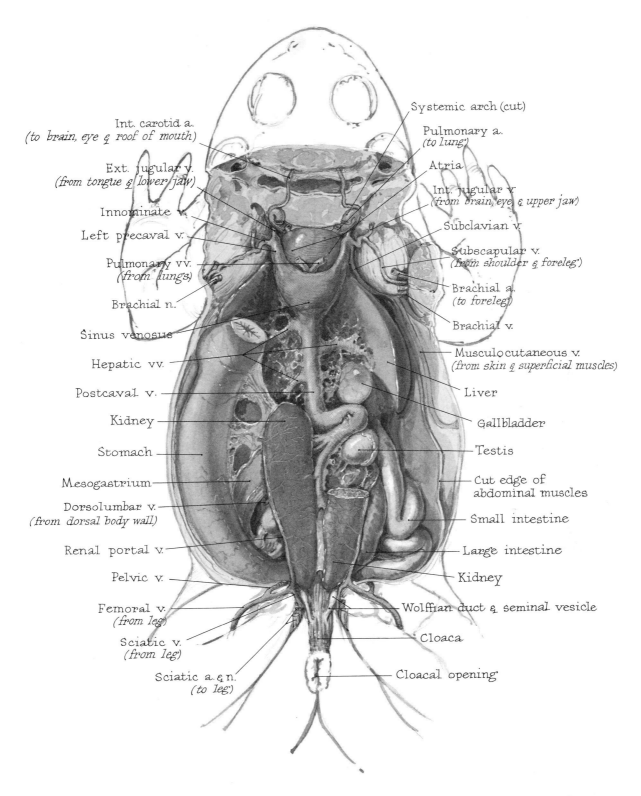

Int. carotid a.
(to brain, eye & roof of mouth)

Ext. jugular v.
(from tongue & lower jaw)

Innominate v.

Left precaval v.

Pulmonary vv.
(from lungs)

Brachial n.

Sinus venosus

Hepatic vv.

Postcaval v.

Kidney

Stomach

Mesogastrium

Dorsolumbar v.
(from dorsal body wall)

Renal portal v.

Pelvic v.

Femoral v.
(from leg)

Sciatic v.
(from leg)

Sciatic a. & n.
(to leg)

Systemic arch (cut)

Pulmonary a.
(to lung)

Atria

Int. jugular v.
(from brain, eye & upper jaw)

Subclavian v.

Subscapular v.
(from shoulder & foreleg)

Brachial a.
(to foreleg)

Brachial v.

Musculocutaneous v.
(from skin & superficial muscles)

Liver

Gallbladder

Testis

Cut edge of
abdominal muscles

Small intestine

Large intestine

Kidney

Wolffian duct & seminal vesicle

Cloaca

Cloacal opening

The esophagus, dorsal aorta, fat bodies, and part of the right kidney are removed, and the liver is partially dissected to show the postcaval vein and the hepatic veins. On the right the muscles of the abdominal wall are cut to show the musculocutaneous vein, which lies just under the skin. On the left the subclavian and musculocutaneous veins are concealed by the liver and stomach.

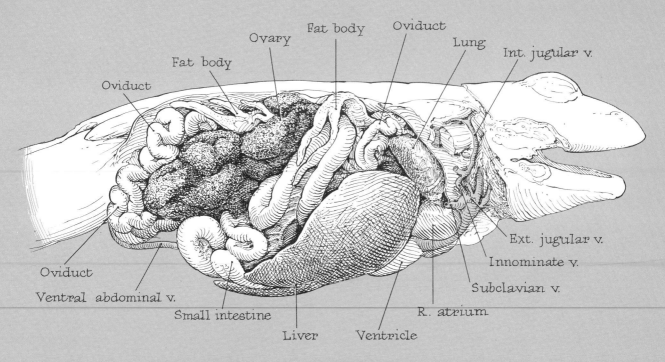

Oviduct · Fat body · Ovary · Fat body · Oviduct · Lung · Int. jugular v.

Oviduct · Ventral abdominal v. · Small intestine · Liver · Ventricle · R. atrium · Subclavian v. · Innominate v. · Ext. jugular v.

RIGHT LATERAL VIEW OF THE VISCERA IN A FEMALE SPECIMEN

The ovaries are distended with ova and the oviducts are distended with the jelly which will coat the eggs. Most of the oviduct is concealed by the ovary and the fat body.

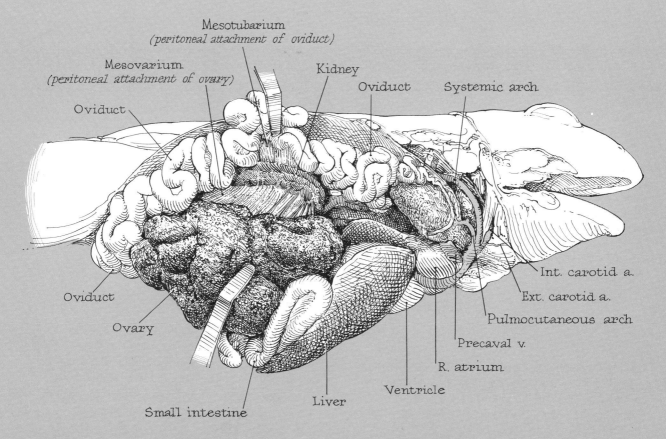

Mesotubarium
(peritoneal attachment of oviduct)

Mesovarium
(peritoneal attachment of ovary)

Oviduct · Kidney · Oviduct · Systemic arch

Oviduct · Ovary · Small intestine · Liver · Ventricle · R. atrium · Precaval v. · Pulmocutaneous arch · Ext. carotid a. · Int. carotid a.

The fat body is removed and the ovary and oviduct are retracted to show their peritoneal attachments.

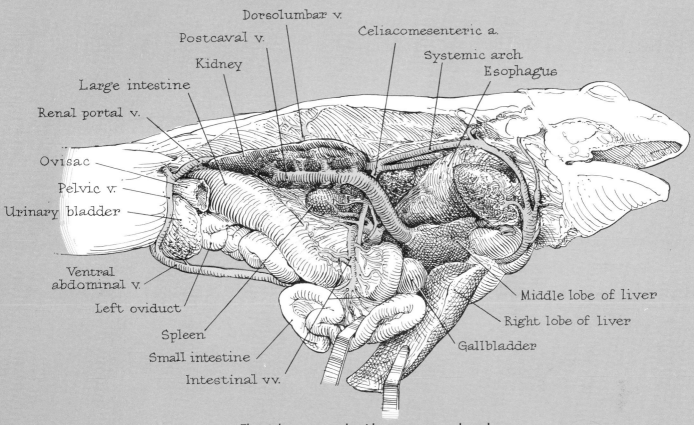

Dorsolumbar v.

Postcaval v.

Kidney

Celiacomesenteric a.

Systemic arch

Esophagus

Large intestine

Renal portal v.

Ovisac

Pelvic v.

Urinary bladder

Ventral abdominal v.

Left oviduct

Spleen

Small intestine

Intestinal vv.

Middle lobe of liver

Right lobe of liver

Gallbladder

The right ovary and oviduct are removed, and
the small intestine and liver are retracted to show
the course of the intestinal veins and the celiacomesenteric artery.

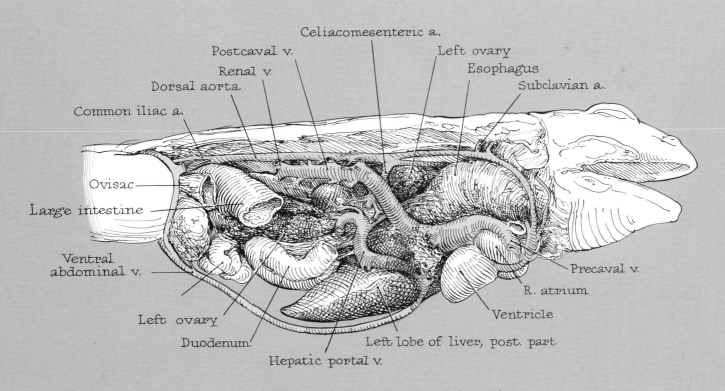

Celiacomesenteric a.

Postcaval v.

Renal v.

Dorsal aorta

Common iliac a.

Left ovary

Esophagus

Subclavian a.

Ovisac

Large intestine

Ventral abdominal v.

Precaval v.

R. atrium

Left ovary

Duodenum

Hepatic portal v.

Left lobe of liver, post. part

Ventricle

The right kidney, the small intestine, and most of
the large intestine are removed. The right lobe of
the liver is removed and the liver is partially dissected to show the course of the postcaval vein
and hepatic portal vein.

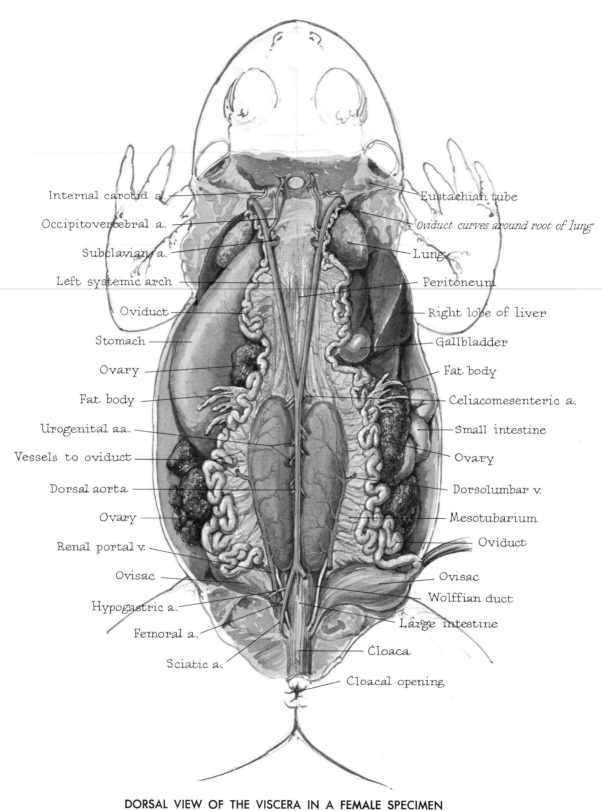

Internal carotid a.
Occipitovertebral a.
Subclavian a.
Left systemic arch
Oviduct
Stomach
Ovary
Fat body
Urogenital aa.
Vessels to oviduct
Dorsal aorta
Ovary
Renal portal v.
Ovisac
Hypogastric a.
Femoral a.
Sciatic a.

Eustachian tube
Oviduct curves around root of lung
Lung
Peritoneum
Right lobe of liver
Gallbladder
Fat body
Celiacomesenteric a.
Small intestine
Ovary
Dorsolumbar v.
Mesotubarium
Oviduct
Ovisac
Wolffian duct
Large intestine
Cloaca
Cloacal opening

DORSAL VIEW OF THE VISCERA IN A FEMALE SPECIMEN

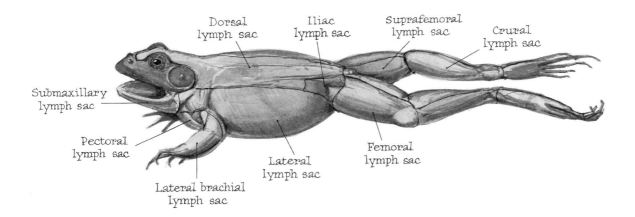

Dorsal lymph sac · Iliac lymph sac · Suprafemoral lymph sac · Crural lymph sac · Submaxillary lymph sac · Pectoral lymph sac · Lateral brachial lymph sac · Lateral lymph sac · Femoral lymph sac

THE LYMPHATIC SYSTEM

The frog's skin is loosely attached to the body by septa of connective tissue which form partitions between the subcutaneous lymph spaces. These spaces communicate with each other by means of small oval openings in the septa. Water and certain foodstuffs may be absorbed into the subcutaneous spaces through the skin, and water may also be lost through the skin. A frog kept in dry air for some time may lose as much as 40 per cent of its weight by dessication, but regain its plumpness and vigor when returned to water.

In addition to the subcutaneous lymph spaces, there is a variety of deep lymph spaces in all parts of the body. The largest of these is the subvertebral lymph space (illustrated on page 25). It contains the kidneys and extends along most of the dorsal body cavity.

Lymph, which consists of blood plasma minus most of the blood proteins, forms an internal environment through which all materials exchanged between the blood and the cells diffuse. It filters through the capillary walls to fill the coelom and the lymph spaces. From the coelom it is returned to the venous circulation by the nephrostomes, minute ciliated openings on the ventral surface of the kidneys. The cilia create a current of lymph from the coelom into the nephrostomes, which connect with branches of the renal veins. Lymph is returned from the deep and subcutaneous spaces by four lymph hearts. They are small endothelial sacs encircled by striated muscle and connective tissue. The two posterior lymph hearts lie on either side of the urostyle, and their pulsations can be observed in an anesthetized frog if the skin over

the urostyle is removed. The anterior lymph hearts cannot be seen from the dorsal view. They lie near the transverse process of the third vertebra and are covered by muscle. The posterior lymph hearts empty into the transverse iliac vein, a connecting vein between the femoral vein and the sciatic vein. The anterior lymph hearts empty into the vertebral vein, a branch of the internal jugular vein.

Whereas carbohydrates and proteins enter the circulation via the intestinal capillaries, fats enter via intestinal lymphatics which lead back through the mesentery to empty into the subvertebral lymph space. Lymph circulates much more slowly than blood, and, therefore, the pressure in the lymphatics is lower than it is in the capillaries. It is thought that because of their relatively greater size, fat molecules pass more readily into lymphatics than into capillaries, since lymphatics are more permeable to molecules of large size than are capillaries.

The lymphatics are more highly developed in tetrapods than they are in fish. The absence of gills and gill capillaries in the arterial circuit makes possible the higher blood pressure and more rapid circulation which enable tetrapods to meet the demands of an active terrestrial life. It is thought that the development of the lymphatics in tetrapods may serve the function of providing a low-pressure return channel for tissue liquids which cannot enter capillaries against pressure.

In amphibians the volume of lymph and the speed of its circulation are much greater than in other tetrapods. One study showed that the lymph hearts of a frog pump a volume of lymph equal to fifty times the total amount of blood plasma each day.

THE REPRODUCTIVE ORGANS

Frogs breed once a year. In the early spring, just after hibernation, they migrate to ponds and slow-moving streams in great numbers. The time of breeding varies considerably, depending on the latitude and the temperature. Warm weather generally hastens the time of breeding, while cool weather retards it.

Usually the males precede the females by a few days and take up stations from which they call to attract mates. When approached by another frog, the male climbs onto its back and grasps it firmly just behind the forelegs in the mating embrace termed *amplexus*. This clasping reflex is one of the strongest instincts of the male frog. During the breeding season he may indiscriminately clasp another male, a female of another species, a fish, or almost any other object which comes within reach. However, objects other than female frogs are shortly released, as are females which have already laid their eggs. The factors which enable the male frog to distinguish the sex of a female and to ejaculate at the moment of oviposition are complex and vary from species to species.*

When a male succeeds in mounting a suitable female he tenaciously maintains his hold until the eggs are laid. Under normal conditions this will often occur within a few days of the time amplexus commences, but cold weather may prolong the period of amplexus for several weeks. The male discharges his sperm over the eggs as they are laid, and the frogs then separate to resume their solitary lives. Generally several thousand eggs are laid at a time. The number of eggs varies considerably from species to species: *R. pipiens,* the leopard frog, lays 2,000 to 3,000 eggs, while *R. catesbeiana,* the bullfrog, is reported to have laid as many as 20,000 eggs. The vast majority of the eggs and tadpoles, of course, are destined to furnish food for predators such as fish, birds, snakes, and turtles.

A number of important seasonal changes take place in connection with mating. As breeding season approaches, the foreleg muscles which the male uses in amplexus undergo hypertrophy, as does a swelling on the inner side of his first finger. This swelling apparently helps the male maintain his grasp during amplexus. In some species, small dermal papillae develop on the back and sides of the female during breeding season. These papillae are thought to provide a tactile stimulus in connection with mating.

In the spring just after mating, the ovaries are small and shriveled. During the summer they increase in size as eggs develop within them, until by fall they fill most of the body cavity. Glands within the oviducts secrete a gelatinous material which forms the coverings of the eggs. The presence of this gelatinous material within the oviducts accounts for their distention in specimens containing large ovaries. In specimens with small or medium-sized ovaries the oviducts are proportionately smaller.

The fat bodies provide a reserve supply of nutriment used during the reproductive processes. They are necessary for maintaining the health and normal development of the gonads. During summer the fat bodies increase in size as nutriment is stored in them. In the spring, before and during mating, their reserves are consumed and they shrink greatly. Compare the fat bodies of the specimens illustrated on pages 36 and 40.

After the male has mounted the female, the eggs break through the ovarian follicles and are discharged into the coelom. They are conveyed toward the anterior end of the coelom by the action of cilia on the inner surface of the peritoneum and are taken into the funnel-shaped mouths (*ostia*) of the oviducts, which open into the coelom near the ventral side of the base of the lung. The eggs then pass single file down the lumen of the oviduct, propelled by cilia on the ridges of the inner walls. Between the ridges are the openings of glands which secrete a gelatinous material, and as the eggs pass through the oviducts they receive protective coats of jelly. Eggs which have passed down the oviduct are retained in the ovisac until ovulation is complete. The eggs are then extruded from the cloaca and fertilized. On coming into contact with water, the jelly swells greatly to form a transparent coat which protects the egg against damage, against fungus and other infections, and also acts as an insulator to prevent heat loss.

* Chapter 9 of Maxwell R. Savage's *Ecology and Life History of the Common Frog* (London: Sir Isaac Pitman & Sons, 1961) contains an interesting discussion of these factors, together with references to recent papers on the subject.

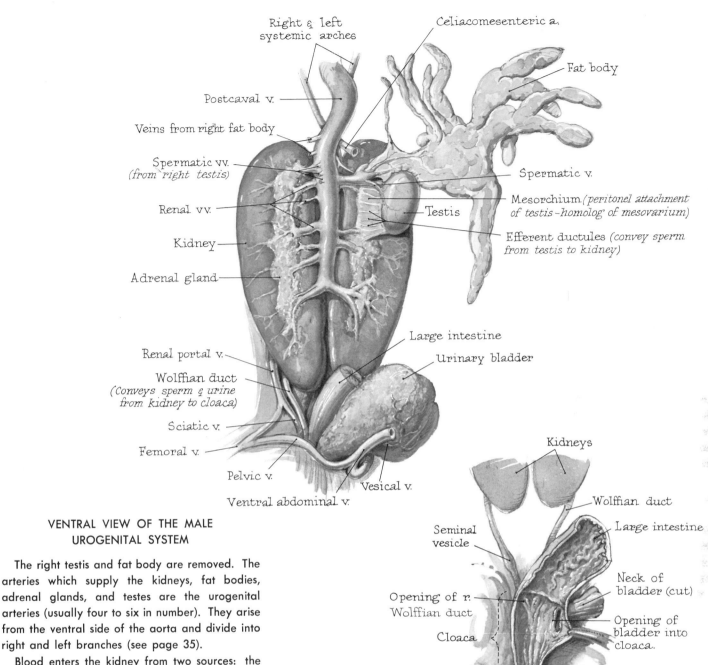

Right & left systemic arches

Celiacomesenteric a.

Fat body

Postcaval v.

Veins from right fat body

Spermatic vv. *(from right testis)*

Renal vv.

Kidney

Adrenal gland

Spermatic v.

Mesorchium *(peritonel attachment of testis - homolog of mesovarium)*

Testis

Efferent ductules *(convey sperm from testis to kidney)*

Large intestine

Urinary bladder

Renal portal v.

Wolffian duct *(Conveys sperm & urine from kidney to cloaca)*

Sciatic v.

Femoral v.

Pelvic v.

Ventral abdominal v.

Vesical v.

Kidneys

Wolffian duct

Large intestine

Seminal vesicle

Opening of r. Wolffian duct

Cloaca

Neck of bladder (cut)

Opening of bladder into cloaca.

VENTRAL VIEW OF THE MALE UROGENITAL SYSTEM

The right testis and fat body are removed. The arteries which supply the kidneys, fat bodies, adrenal glands, and testes are the urogenital arteries (usually four to six in number). They arise from the ventral side of the aorta and divide into right and left branches (see page 35).

Blood enters the kidney from two sources: the urogenital arteries and the renal portal vein. Blood from both sources passes through capillaries around the nephrons and returns via the renal veins to the postcava. The nephrons are microscopic tubules which constitute the functional units of the kidney. They regulate blood volume and composition; they also excrete metabolic wastes, which filter through the capillary walls and pass from the nephrons into transverse collecting tubules which carry them to the Wolffian ducts.

Although the course of the spermatozoa through the kidney varies in different species of frogs, in general it may be said that the spermatozoa pass from the testes through the *efferent ductules* to the same collecting tubules into which the nephrons empty. Thus the spermatozoa and the urine follow the same course through the collecting tubules and the Wolffian ducts to the cloaca.

THE CLOACA

The pelvic girdle is cut and the cloaca is opened by a cut along the right side. The bladder opens into the ventral side of the cloaca opposite the openings of the Wolffian ducts.

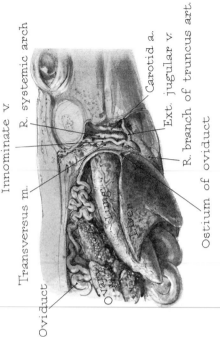

Innominate v.

R. systemic arch

Transversus m.

Carotid a.

Ext. jugular v.

R. branch of truncus art.

Ostium of oviduct

Oviduct

CRANIAL PORTION OF THE RIGHT OVIDUCT, LATERAL VIEW

The walls of the ovary are folded upon each other and the inner cavity is divided into several compartments. It is covered by a layer of peritoneum which suspends it from the body wall by a double fold termed the *mesovarium* (homolog of the mesorchium). The convoluted shape of the ovarian walls enables all the eggs which develop within its follicles to lie close to the surface. During ovulation, the eggs break through the peritoneal covering of the ovary to enter the coelom. The ostia of the oviducts, through which all the eggs pass on their way to the ovisacs, lie on either side of the heart just medial to the small peritoneal band connecting the lateral edge of the liver with the parietal peritoneum.

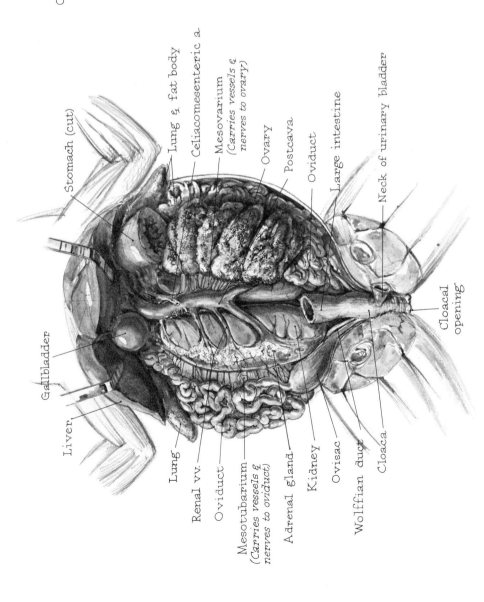

Stomach (cut)

Lung & fat body

Celiacomesenteric a.

Mesovarium
(*Carries vessels & nerves to ovary*)

Ovary

Postcava

Oviduct

Large intestine

Neck of urinary bladder

Gallbladder

Liver

Lung

Renal vv.

Oviduct

Mesotubarium
(*Carries vessels & nerves to oviduct*)

Adrenal gland

Kidney

Ovisac

Wolffian duct

Cloaca

Cloacal opening

FEMALE UROGENITAL SYSTEM, VENTRAL VIEW

Most of the alimentary canal, together with the right ovary and fat body, are removed. The legs and pelvic girdle are cut to reveal the cloaca.

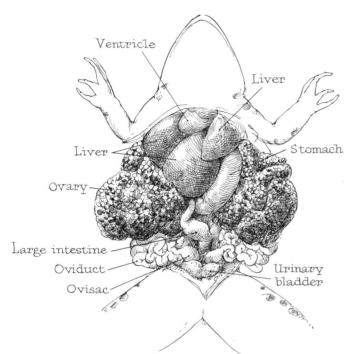

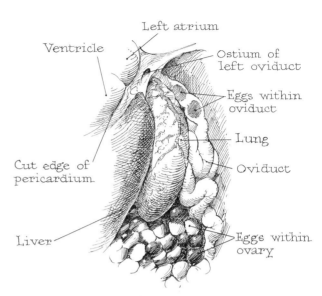

Before ovulation the eggs lie within follicles in the ovarian walls and the oviducts are swollen with jelly.

As ovulation begins, the first eggs are discharged from the ovaries into the body cavity and carried toward the ostium of the oviduct by the action of peritoneal cilia.

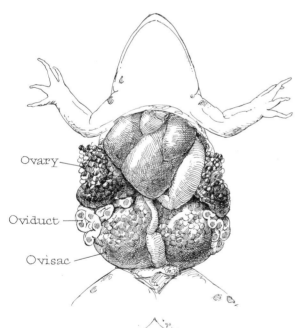

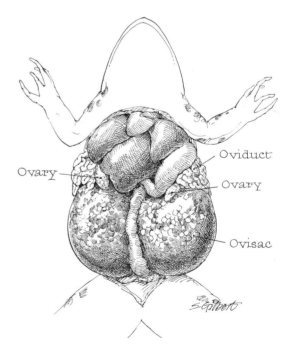

As the eggs move through the oviducts into the ovisacs, the ovaries shrink and the ovisacs become distended. Within the oviducts the eggs receive their gelatinous coats.

After ovulation is complete the ovisacs fill most of the body cavity and the ovaries are reduced to a small fraction of their former size.

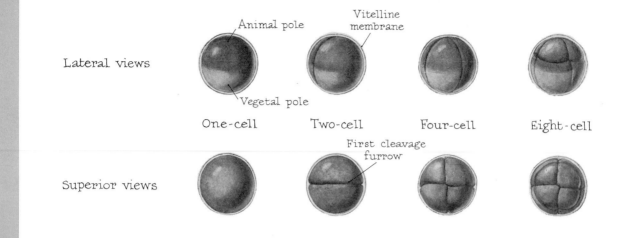

Lateral views

Animal pole

Vitelline membrane

Vegetal pole

One-cell   Two-cell   Four-cell   Eight-cell

First cleavage furrow

Superior views

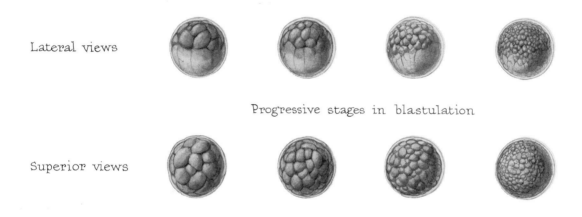

Lateral views

Progressive stages in blastulation

Superior views

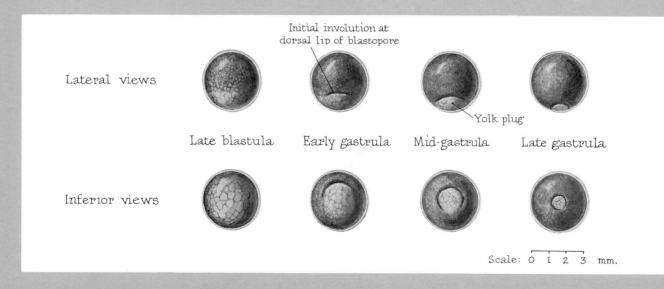

Initial involution at dorsal lip of blastopore

Lateral views

Yolk plug

Late blastula   Early gastrula   Mid-gastrula   Late gastrula

Inferior views

Scale: 0 1 2 3 mm.

DEVELOPMENT OF THE FROG'S EGG
(Rana aurora)

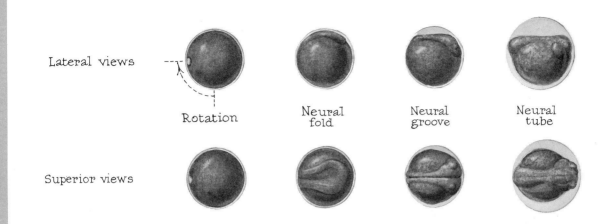

Lateral views

Rotation · Neural fold · Neural groove · Neural tube

Superior views

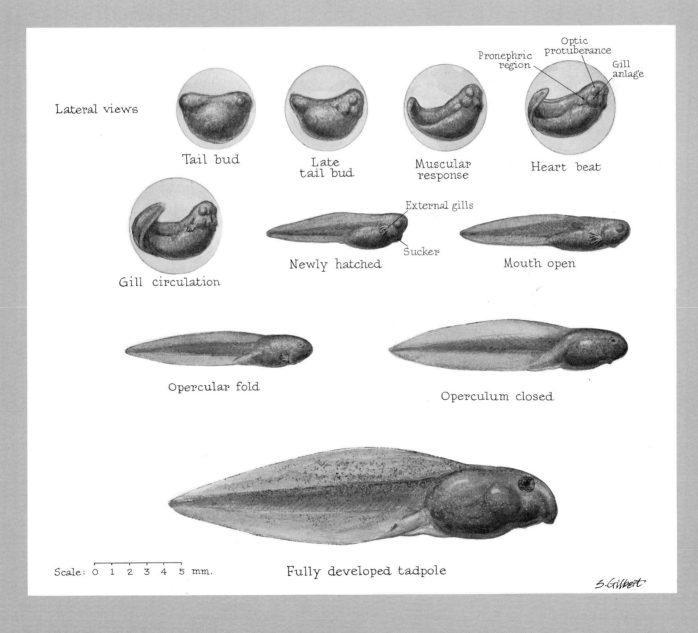

Lateral views

Tail bud · Late tail bud · Muscular response · Heart beat

Pronephric region · Optic protuberance · Gill anlage

Gill circulation

Newly hatched · External gills · Sucker · Mouth open

Opercular fold

Operculum closed

Scale: 0 1 2 3 4 5 mm.

Fully developed tadpole

S. Gilbert

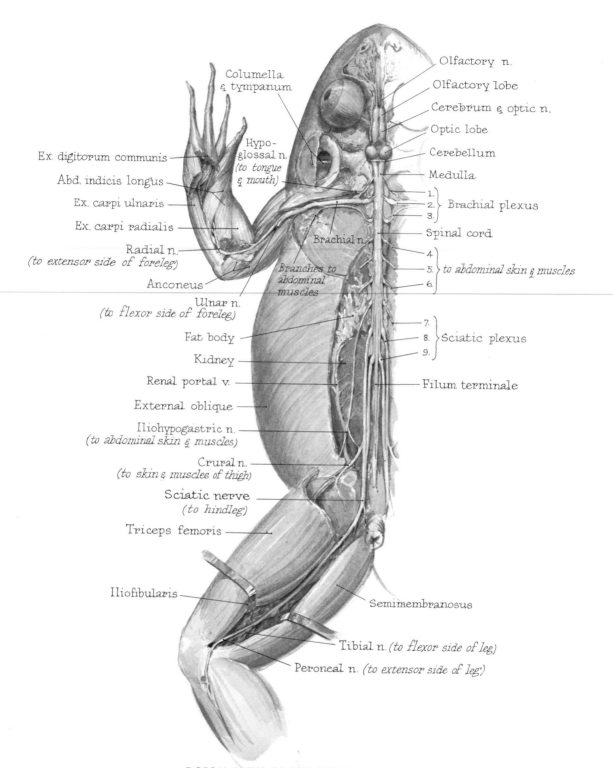

Columella & tympanum

Ex. digitorum communis

Abd. indicis longus

Ex. carpi ulnaris

Ex. carpi radialis

Radial n.
(to extensor side of foreleg)

Anconeus

Hypo-
glossal n.
*(to tongue
& mouth)*

Ulnar n.
(to flexor side of foreleg)

Fat body

Kidney

Renal portal v.

External oblique

Iliohypogastric n.
(to abdominal skin & muscles)

Crural n.
(to skin & muscles of thigh)

Sciatic nerve
(to hindleg)

Triceps femoris

Iliofibularis

Olfactory n.

Olfactory lobe

Cerebrum & optic n.

Optic lobe

Cerebellum

Medulla

1.
2.   } Brachial plexus
3.

Spinal cord

Brachial n.

Branches to
abdominal
muscles

4.
5.   } to abdominal skin & muscles
6.

7.
8.   } Sciatic plexus
9.

Filum terminale

Semimembranosus

Tibial n. *(to flexor side of leg)*

Peroneal n. *(to extensor side of leg)*

DORSAL VIEW OF THE NERVOUS SYSTEM

The dorsal walls of the skull and vertebral column are removed to reveal the brain and spinal cord. The tenth spinal nerve, not visible from the dorsal view, emerges near the anterior end of the urostyle. It joins a branch of the ninth nerve to form the ischiococcygeal plexus, which gives branches to the bladder, coaca, oviducts, and posterior lymph hearts.

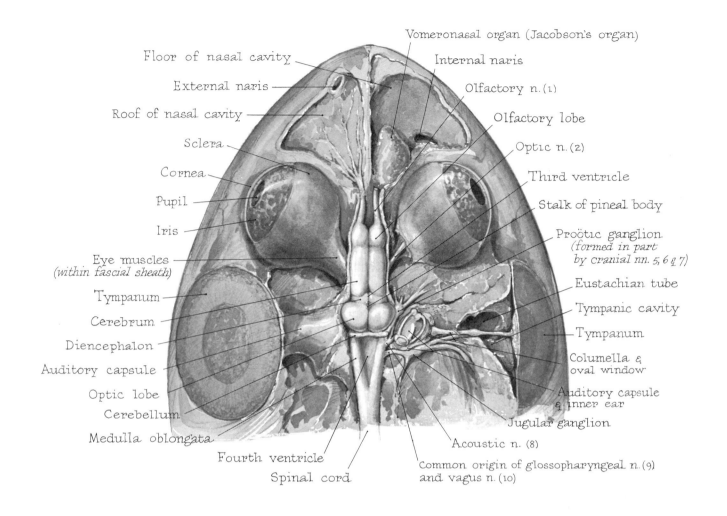

Floor of nasal cavity

External naris

Roof of nasal cavity

Sclera

Cornea

Pupil

Iris

Eye muscles
(within fascial sheath)

Tympanum

Cerebrum

Diencephalon

Auditory capsule

Optic lobe

Cerebellum

Medulla oblongata

Fourth ventricle

Spinal cord

Vomeronasal organ (Jacobson's organ)

Internal naris

Olfactory n. (1)

Olfactory lobe

Optic n. (2)

Third ventricle

Stalk of pineal body

Proötic ganglion
(formed in part
by cranial nn. 5, 6 & 7)

Eustachian tube

Tympanic cavity

Tympanum

Columella &
oval window

Auditory capsule
& inner ear

Jugular ganglion

Acoustic n. (8)

Common origin of glossopharyngeal n. (9)
and vagus n. (10)

DORSAL VIEW OF THE HEAD AND BRAIN

The top of the skull is removed. On the left, the roof of the nasal cavity, the eye muscles, and the auditory capsule are intact. On the right, the dissection is carried deeper to show some of the cranial nerves; the roof of the nasal cavity is removed, the eye muscles are cut, and the auditory capsule is opened to reveal the inner ear.

In the frog there are two protective membranes around the central nervous system. They are the *dura mater,* a thin membrane which adheres to the bone (that part of the *dura mater* lying dorsal to the brain is removed with the top of the skull), and the *pia mater,* a vascular membrane which lies close to the surface of the brain and spinal cord. Over the third and fourth ventricles the *pia mater* fuses with a thin layer of epithelium to form the *choroid plexuses,* highly vascularized tufts which hang down into the ventricles. Exchange of nutrient substances and other materials takes place between the blood and the cerebrospinal fluid through the *choroid plexuses.*

In the center of the diencephalon is the small stalk of the pineal body. The pineal body itself usually adheres to the roof of the skull and is torn off when the cranium is opened. This is the rudiment of a primitive third eye possessed by early vertebrates but lost in the course of evolution. The external vestige of the third eye may be seen in many frogs as a tiny white fleck embedded in the skin between the eyes.

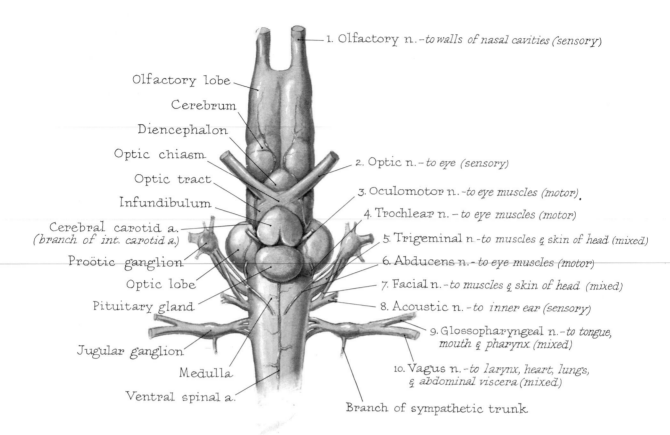

1. Olfactory n.–*to walls of nasal cavities (sensory)*

Olfactory lobe

Cerebrum

Diencephalon

Optic chiasm

Optic tract

Infundibulum

Cerebral carotid a.
(branch of int. carotid a.)

Proötic ganglion

Optic lobe

Pituitary gland

Jugular ganglion

Medulla

Ventral spinal a.

2. Optic n.–*to eye (sensory)*

3. Oculomotor n.–*to eye muscles (motor)*

4. Trochlear n.–*to eye muscles (motor)*

5. Trigeminal n.–*to muscles & skin of head (mixed)*

6. Abducens n.–*to eye muscles (motor)*

7. Facial n.–*to muscles & skin of head (mixed)*

8. Acoustic n.–*to inner ear (sensory)*

9. Glossopharyngeal n.–*to tongue, mouth & pharynx (mixed)*

10. Vagus n.–*to larynx, heart, lungs, & abdominal viscera (mixed)*

Branch of sympathetic trunk

VENTRAL VIEW OF THE BRAIN

The central nervous system originates as a tube with a central cavity which develops into the ventricles of the brain and the central canal of the spinal cord. Within these cavities and also surrounding the spinal cord and brain is the cerebrospinal fluid, a slowly circulating, lymphlike substance which forms a protective liquid cushion for the central nervous system.

The pituitary gland (or hypophysis) lies within a depression in the floor of the skull and is usually left in the skull when the brain is removed. It is one of the most important of the endocrine glands, producing hormones which influence growth and control the actions of the other hormone-producing glands in addition to acting directly on a variety of body tissues.

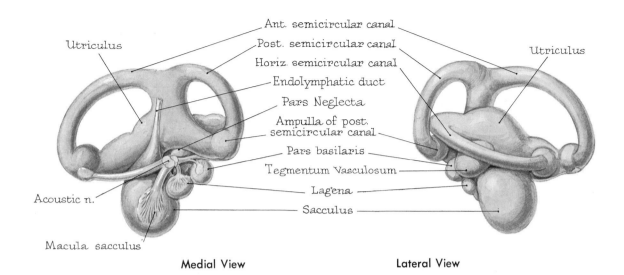

Utriculus · Ant. semicircular canal · Post. semicircular canal · Horiz. semicircular canal · Endolymphatic duct · Pars Neglecta · Ampulla of post. semicircular canal · Pars basilaris · Tegmentum Vasculosum · Lagena · Sacculus · Utriculus · Acoustic n. · Macula sacculus

Medial View   Lateral View

THE INNER EAR

In mammals the eardrum lies at the end of the external auditory canal. In the frog, however, the eardrum (tympanum) lies on the surface of the head, and there is no external auditory canal or external ear.

The cavity of the middle ear connects with the mouth via the Eustachian tube and is closed externally by the tympanum, which responds to vibrations in the air. These vibrations are conveyed to the inner ear by the columella. The medial end of the columella articulates with a plug of cartilage which fits into the oval window, a small opening in the auditory capsule. In the mammalian middle ear, there is an articulated chain of three ossicles, the stapes, incus, and malleus. It is usually said that the stapes is the homolog of the columella, while the homologs of the malleus and incus are present in the frog as articulating portions of the upper and lower jaws.*

The inner ear, or membranous labyrinth, is a minute system of sacs and canals which lies within the auditory capsule. It is filled with a fluid, the endolymph, and surrounded by another fluid, the perilymph. The three canals lie in mutually perpendicular planes. The sacs contain masses of calcium carbonate crystals termed otoliths. Changes in the positions of the otoliths are perceived by sensory patches, or maculae, and this enables the frog to maintain its equilibrium. Sensory areas within the ampullae at the ends of the canals are thought to register changes in motion.

According to Gaupp it is the utriculus, sacculus, and lagena which contain otoliths and function (along with the semicircular canals) to register changes in position and motion. He ascribes auditory functions only to the *pars basilaris* and the *pars neglecta* (termed *recessus papillae amphibiorum* by later authors).

In the frog, the inner ear is mainly an organ of equilibration. In mammals, sound is perceived in the cochlea, a coiled tube which often constitutes the largest part of the inner ear. The cochlea has evolved from the lagena, the nerve ending in the *pars basilaris,* and the perilymphatic duct (a lymph-filled canal which conveys vibrations from the oval window to the *pars basilaris*). The frog is descended from a vertebrate ancestor in which the part of the inner ear specialized for the reception of sound was still in a rudimentary stage of development.

An unusual feature of the frog's inner ear is the extensive ramification of the endolymphatic duct. It passes from the sacculus through a foramen in the auditory capsule to form a connection with a system of endolymphatic sacs which surround the brain and spinal cord, lying between the dura and the pia mater. Secretions formed by this system of sacs can be seen as the knobby, chalklike deposits (calcareous bodies) found at the base of the brain and on either side of the vertebral column surrounding the exits of the spinal nerves. These deposits consist of the same calcium carbonate crystals which form the otoliths. They have no apparent functional significance.

* This interpretation has been contested by Tumarkin (1955), who says that the relationship is one of analogy rather than homology.

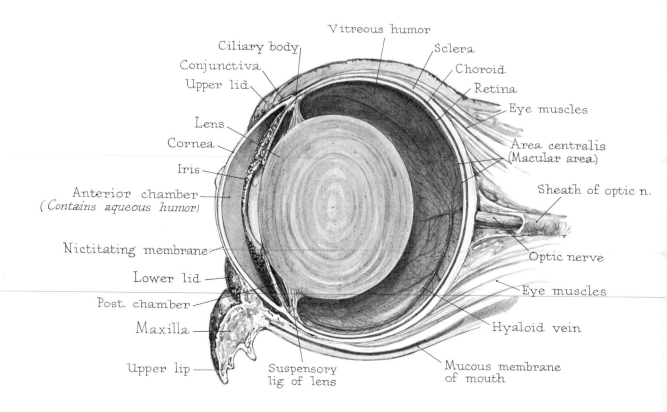

Vitreous humor
Ciliary body
Conjunctiva
Upper lid
Sclera
Choroid
Retina
Eye muscles
Lens
Cornea
Iris
Anterior chamber
(*Contains aqueous humor*)
Area centralis
(Macular area)
Sheath of optic n.
Nictitating membrane
Lower lid
Optic nerve
Post. chamber
Eye muscles
Maxilla
Hyaloid vein
Upper lip
Suspensory
lig. of lens
Mucous membrane
of mouth

THE EYE

Perhaps the most striking feature of the eyes as observed superficially in the living frog is that instead of being protected by a bony socket like the eyes of most terrestrial vertebrates, they protrude considerably above the level of the skull. Another interesting feature is that there is very little white showing in the eye of the frog. The cornea, iris, and lens are much larger in relation to the size of the eye than they are in the human. The sclera, or white of the eye, is seen only as a very thin strip near the edge of the lid in the frog. The eyes are large in relation to the brain (see page 49) and in cross-section are seen to extend from the roof of the mouth to the top of the head.

For protection, the eyes are withdrawn into the orbit, causing prominent bulges in the roof of the mouth. The lids have no power of independent movement, but close passively over the eye when it is withdrawn. The surface of the eye is kept moist and clean by an extension of the lower lid, the nictitating membrane. (This structure, also termed the *palpebral spectacle,* is not homologous with the nictitating membrane of amniotes.) Eye

movements, which are minimal in the frog, are effected by muscles which arise from the skull and are inserted on the external tunic of the eye. There are four rectus muscles (superior, inferior, anterior, and posterior) which turn the eye upward, downward, forward, and backward, respectively. The superior oblique muscle turns the upper margin of the eye forward and downward, while the inferior oblique produces the opposite effect. The *retractor bulbi* muscle pulls the eye into the orbit. The *levator bulbi,* a flat muscle which forms the floor of the orbit, pushes the eye outward.

The external tunic of the eye is a rigid protective layer consisting of the sclera and the cornea. The sclera, which constitutes the medial two thirds of the surface, is an opaque white covering composed of hyaline cartilage and connective tissue. The cornea covers the lateral third of the sphere and is the transparent portion of the external tunic through which light enters the eye. Beneath the sclera lies the choroid, a vascular membrane which carries nutriment for the retina. The choroid is heavily pigmented and absorbs most of the light which passes through the retina, thus preventing the confusion of images which would result from the internal reflection of light.

The retina, or photoreceptive inner tunic of the eye, is composed of nervous and sensory elements which respond to visual stimuli. Analysis of optic nerve impulses in *Rana* indicates that the retina responds to selected patterns of stimuli which are significant in terms of the frog's mode of life. Separate impulses are triggered by the following characteristics of visual stimuli: contrast, convexity, velocity of a moving edge, reduction of illumination, darkness, and blue light.

The sensory portion of the retina consists of both rod and cone cells, and there is an *area centralis* where cones are more numerous than elsewhere. This is the area of most acute vision. It is generally said that rod cells function in the perception of faint light and give poorly defined black-and-white images, while the less numerous cone cells function only under good illumination, give better visual details, and, in some animals, respond to color. Frogs are capable of distinguishing blue from other colors, but probably do not experience color vision as we know it.

The anterior portions of the choroid and retina (minus its sensory components) combine to form the iris. It contains muscle fibers which regulate the amount of light admitted to the eye by changing the size of the pupil. These muscles respond to autonomic nervous control, and a direct response to light has also been demonstrated in the iris of the isolated eye. Embryologically, the muscle fibers of the iris arise from its retinal component, which, like the rest of the nervous system, develops from the neural ectoderm of the embryo. The muscle fibers of the iris are unique in that they are the only known muscle to derive from ectoderm; all other muscles originate from mesoderm.

The transparent lens, which is composed of concentric layers of elongated cells lying parallel to the optical axis, acts together with the cornea to bring the rays of light entering the eye to a focus on the retina. The lens can be moved forward to accommodate for nearby objects. In contrast, teleosts move the lens backwards to accommodate for distant objects, and amniotes accommodate by modifying the shape of the lens.

In the frog, as in other lower vertebrates (lampreys through birds) all the fibers of the optic nerves cross at the optic chiasm and go to the side of the brain opposite the eye from which they originate. In mammals, however, this crossing is incomplete; some fibers from the left sides of both retinas go to the left side of the brain and vice versa, with the result that sensations from retinal areas which perceive a common binocular image go to the same side of the brain. The significance of the incomplete crossing of optic nerve fibers in mammals is not entirely clear. It is thought to be connected with stereoscopic depth perception and/or with the fact that in mammals voluntary eye movements are coordinated so that both eyes are always directed toward a common point in space. (This is not the case in nonmammalian forms, many of which are capable of moving one eye independently of the other.) Whether or not lower vertebrates experience stereoscopic depth perceptions like our own is a matter of debate. The frog does have a field of binocular vision which enables it to see objects directly ahead with both eyes simultaneously, and the fact that a frog can leap at and capture flying insects in midair with consistently good aim demonstrates that, whatever its subjective sensations may be, the frog is able to judge distances quite accurately.

The frog's eye may be compared to a camera with a wide-angle lens which has a short focal length, takes in a large field of view, enlarges images of nearby objects, and reduces images of distant objects. The wide field of view and the protrusion of the eyes above the head enable the frog to perceive prey or predators approaching from almost any direction while it is lying motionless in ambush or floating with only its eyes above the surface of the water. The relatively large cornea together with the potentially wide pupil and the nearly spherical lens (characteristics shared by nocturnal and aquatic animals) enable the eye to gather a maximum amount of light. This facilitates vision at night, when many frogs are most active. The fact that the lens forms large images of nearby objects and moves forward to accommodate for close-up vision affords the frog a good view of small animals which come within snapping distance.

The frog does not have good distance vision. The visual cells are relatively large, and this, combined with the fact that the lens forms small images of distant objects, probably results in a subjective sensation analogous to what we see in a very small photo reproduced by coarse halftone dots. The frog, however, leads a life in which the distinct perception of distant objects is not essential. It does not pursue its prey, but waits in ambush until the prey comes within snapping distance. Any large moving object is a signal for the frog to flee or hide.

The frog's eye seems to be a structure which, though originally evolved for underwater vision, has been adapted to use in the air with relatively little change. The eye of the fish is similar to that of the frog except that the lens is even more nearly spherical and lies closer to the cornea. Most fish, like frogs, can turn their heads only slightly. For them, maximum light-gathering power and a wide field of view are essential in an underwater environment where light is often dim and predators approach noiselessly. The ability to see distant objects distinctly is of little value to fish because light does not carry far underwater.

For most terrestrial vertebrates which are active by day, the ability to distinguish prey and predators at the greatest possible distance is essential for survival. In such animals the lens is typically of long focal length, which makes distant objects appear larger than they appear to the frog. Such a lens, together with good retinal resolving power, give these animals superior visual acuity. A freely moveable neck compensates for the loss of a wide visual field by enabling the eyes to scan a landscape or turn quickly toward any noise which may signal the approach of a predator.

Dissecting Instructions

The purpose of your reading and dissection should be to form a broad understanding of the ways in which the structure of the frog is related to the demands of its environment and to the structure of other vertebrates. The knowledge of some anatomical terminology is necessary as a basis for this understanding, but memorizing the name of every branch of each artery, nerve, and vein should not be mistaken for the study of biology.

As you make your dissection, compare the structures you find in the frog with the structure of other animals you have studied and try to explain anatomical differences in terms of adaptation to the environment. A few questions are included in the dissecting instructions to indicate lines of inquiry which should be occurring to you during your work. Do not stop to look up the answer to each question as you come to it, but keep the questions in mind and think of similar points which may interest you. Some of the answers will be found in the text. Answers to other questions do not lie within the scope of this book, and some of the questions have no clear-cut answers. They are included to suggest topics you may wish to discuss with your instructor or pursue as independent reading projects.

As you come to each new section of the instructions, read the pages listed at the beginning of the section and also read through the section itself before you start.

THE MUSCLES

Refer to pages 15, 16, 17, and 31.

Place the frog on its back in the dissecting pan. With your scissors, make a midventral cut in the skin from the jaw to the cloacal opening. Extend the cut along the ventral surface of the limbs and remove the skin, being careful to cut around the eyes and tympanic membranes without damaging them. Observe that the skin does not adhere closely to the muscles, but is attached by connective tissue septa. Also observe that the subcutaneous fat deposits usually found in mammals are not present in the frog. Examine one of the connective tissue septa under a dissecting microscope to find the oval openings through which lymph flows between the subcutaneous lymph spaces. Note the intricate network of vessels on the inner surface of the skin. Now refer to page 31 and identify the musculocutaneous vein. Cut this vein at some distance from the point where it passes under the pectoralis muscle and keep the cut end in view so that it can be traced later. Separate the muscles by blunt dissection, working along rather than across the fibers, and being careful not to tear or cut the muscles. Identify the muscles by referring to pages 16 and 17. Refer to the skeleton and establish the approximate origins and insertions of the larger muscles.

At this time the instructor may wish to demonstrate the beating of the posterior lymph hearts by pithing or anesthetizing a frog and removing the skin from either side of the urostyle. The same animal can be used to demonstrate the experiments of Galvani and Mueller which were described in the introduction.

Why are the extensors of the leg and foot stronger than the flexors?

What is the function of the rich cutaneous blood supply? Does the musculocutaneous vein carry oxygenated blood, unoxygenated blood, or mixed blood?

What significance can you ascribe to the large subcutaneous lymph spaces? Are such lymph spaces found in mammals? In fish?

NOTE: The muscle names used in this book are those adopted by Holmes. Other authors sometimes use different names for the same muscles, and the following list of the most frequently encountered synonyms may help you to avoid confusion.*

submaxillary : mylohyoid
palmaris longus : flexor digitorum communis
iliacus externus : gluteus
anterior head of triceps femoris : vastus internus
middle head of triceps femoris : rectus femoris
posterior head of triceps femoris : vastus externus
gracilis major and minor : rectus internus major and minor
iliofibularis : biceps femoris

* The terms listed above are those most frequently found in current texts and laboratory manuals. Gaupp, in some cases, uses still another term and in scientific papers his terminology is often followed. Detailed descriptions of anuran musculature may be found in Dunlap (1960), J. Morph., 106: 1-76, and in Ritland (1955), J. Morph., 97: 215-282.

THE MOUTH

Refer to pages 20 and 21.

Open the mouth as far as possible. If necessary, cut the jaws with bone clippers to obtain adequate exposure. Identify the structures illustrated on page 20. Pass a thin probe through the nares and note the point at which the probe enters the oral cavity. Pierce one of the tympanic membranes and pass a probe through the Eustachian tube into the mouth. Probe the opening of the vocal sacs and determine their size and position. Pull the tongue forward and note its attachment and shape. The illustration on page 27 indicates the extent of its flexibility. An interesting discussion of the mechanism involved in the rapid protrusion and retraction of the tongue is given in the article by Carl Gans cited in the bibliography.

The instructor may wish to make a demonstration dissection of the head and larynx in sagittal section as illustrated on page 20. This gives the best view of the relations of the glottis, vocal cords, larynx, and lungs.

The action of the oral ciliated epithelium may be demonstrated in a pithed frog by scattering the roof of the mouth with carmine grains, which will be seen to move slowly backward into the esophagus.

THE ALIMENTARY CANAL AND ASSOCIATED ORGANS

Refer to pages 22 through 27.

Using your scissors, cut the body wall somewhat to the left of the midline and extend the cut from the cloacal opening to the pectoral girdle, being careful not to damage any of the organs within the body cavity. Now lift the cut edges of the abdominal wall and identify the ventral abdominal vein, which lies in the midline, closely attached to the ventral body wall. Free this vein by cutting the ventral mesentery which attaches it to the body wall and leave the vein intact. Now make a transverse cut in the body wall behind the pectoral girdle and another in the pelvic region. Pin back or cut off the ventral portions of the body wall to expose the body cavity or coelom.

Identify the structures found in the body cavity by referring to pages 22, 24, and 25. If you have a specimen in which the ovaries are distended with eggs, you may wish to remove one of the ovaries

to make identification of the other organs easier. The urinary bladder is usually deflated. It may be filled with water introduced through a small glass tube into the cloaca.

As you identify the organs of the body cavity, observe the condition and size of each. Compare your specimen with those of other students and note the relative sizes of the liver, gonads, oviducts, and fat bodies. Of what significance is the variation in size of these structures? Would such extreme variations be found in the viscera of a mammal? Can you estimate the time of year at which your specimen was taken?

Observe that in the frog the heart and lungs are not separated from the abdominal cavity by a diaphragm as they are in mammals. Pass a probe through the glottis into one lung. Cut open the ventral side of the lung and examine its inner surface. If it is more convenient to remove the lung before cutting it open, you may do so, being careful not to cut the oviduct if your specimen is a female. How does the lung of the frog differ from the mammalian lung? Which is more efficient? Why? How does the frog fill its lungs with air? Does respiration occur at sites other than the lung? Can you explain why a frog can breathe only with its mouth closed, and will die of asphyxiation (under normal conditions of temperature and activity) if the mouth is propped open or if the nares are plugged?

Trace the alimentary canal from the mouth to the large intestine. Cut open a section of the stomach and the small intestine. Note the thick muscular walls of the stomach and observe the difference between the appearance of the mucous membrane in the stomach and in the small intestine. How does this difference reflect the different functions of the stomach and the small intestine? Why is the wall of the stomach so much thicker than the wall of the small intestine? Is this condition found in mammals?

Cut the ventral abdominal vein and raise the liver. Referring to page 26, identify the structures illustrated. Find the point at which the bile duct enters the duodenum by tracing along the inner side of the duodenum. Most of the bile duct lies within the pancreas and can be followed only if the pancreatic tissue is dissected away. In order to trace the course of the bile duct, you will find it helpful to see a demonstration dissection made by your instructor.

Perhaps one of the first things you noticed on

opening the body cavity was that there seems to be a great deal of space around the viscera. In life this space is filled with lymph. Is such a large coelomic space found in mammals? In fish?

Noble says: "The entire blood plasma goes through these portals [the lymph hearts] fifty times a day. The speed of lymph circulation, much greater than in mammals, is a consequence of the greater permeability of the blood vessels in amphibia." Are there other factors which might be connected with the speed of lymph circulation? Might it also be said that the greater permeability of the blood vessels in amphibia is a consequence of the speed of lymph circulation? Can you think of any reasons why the volume and speed of lymph circulation should be greater in the frog than in mammals?

Are any structures analogous to the frog's lymph hearts found in birds or mammals? Are lymphatic vessels or lymph nodes such as those found in mammals present in the frog?

Trace the routes by which lymph returns to the venous circulation from the subcutaneous lymph spaces, the deep lymph spaces, the coelom, and the intestinal lymphatics (see page 41).

If the frog does not store nutriment in subcutaneous fat deposits, how is it able to withstand longer periods of starvation than most mammals can?

Noble says: "Perhaps cold-blooded animals, with their low metabolism, have no need of these stores of potential energy [fat deposits], or perhaps one of the reasons for their never becoming warm-blooded is the leanness of their bodies." Are the two alternatives mutually exclusive? Is this a problem to which a clear-cut answer can be given?

Compare the functions of the stomach, small intestine, and large intestine.

What seems to be the most likely explanation of the fact that carbohydrates and proteins enter the circulation via the intestinal capillaries while fats enter via the intestinal lymphatics?

Where are the digestive enzymes secreted?

What are the constituents of bile?

What are the principal functions of the liver? The spleen? The pancreas?

Holmes reports than "in November the frog's liver may become two and three times as large as it is in June." What is the reason for this?

Can you briefly describe the pioneering experiments of Claude Bernard in determining the functions of the pancreas and liver? An account of his work may be found in *Claude Bernard and*
the Experimental Method in Medicine by Olmsted, J.M.D. and E. Harris Olmsted (New York: Henry Schuman, 1952).

THE CIRCULATORY SYSTEM

Refer to pages 28 through 41.

Turn to page 30 and identify the hepatic portal vein and its branches. Trace it into the liver by picking away the surrounding tissue. Also see the hepatic portal vein as illustrated on pages 26, 28, and 39.

If your specimen is a female, you should identify the ostia of the oviducts at this time so that they will not be accidentally destroyed during the dissection of the circulatory system. Refer to pages 44 and 45 to see the location of the ostia. To find them on your specimen, first identify that portion of the ventral mesentery which attaches the pericardium to the pectoral girdle. Trace along the lateral side of this mesentery with a dull probe and find the ostia near the anterior, or cranial, margin of the liver. You will probably find it convenient to remove some of the pectoral girdle to obtain a good view of the ostia, but do not remove more than necessary at this time. In many specimens the ostia will be difficult to find, and you may need to see a demonstration dissection in order to identify them.

Now refer to page 31 and trace the musculocutaneous vein. Find its union with the brachial vein and identify the subclavian vein lying between the pectoral and abdominal muscles. Using strong scissors or bone clippers and being careful not to damage the heart, cut through the pectoral girdle in the midline. To expose the heart and vessels you may wish to stretch the forelegs apart by pinning them down to the dissecting pan or by tying the feet together with a string or rubber band pulled tight across the back of the frog. Trace the subclavian vein toward the heart on both sides, separating the pectoral muscles from the abdominal muscles as you do so. Open the pericadium and remove it. You are now ready to identify the structures illustrated on page 31. Using a dull probe, forceps, and small scissors, work along the vessels, clearing away the connective tissues and nerves to obtain good definition of the arteries and veins. Remove additional portions of the pectoral girdle as necessary. In order to find the thyroids and parathyroids, you will probably have to use a dissecting microscope and refer to a demonstration dissection.

Refer to page 34 to see the relations of the vessels in the shoulder region. Identify the subclavian artery and nerve and the subscapular vein. Cut these structures on the right side close to the point at which they enter the shoulder muscles. Cut the brachial vein near the point where it passes under the pectoralis major. Remove the right foreleg by cutting through the shoulder muscles, taking care to avoid the previously identified vessels. You may find it convenient at this point to remove the posterior portion of the jaw with bone clippers. This will afford a lateral view of the vessels as illustrated on page 34. After identifying the veins, cut the external jugular, innominate, and subclavian veins at their junction with the precava and remove them, together with portions of the abdominal muscles, to expose the systemic arches. Trace the systemic arches, clearing away nerves, connective tissue, and portions of the petrohyoid muscle as you do so, until you are able to identify all the arteries illustrated on page 34.

In an injected frog, the heart is usually so clogged with latex that it is not practical to study its internal structure. For this purpose you should use a plain preserved or freshly killed frog. Some of the structures within the heart may be difficult for students to identify, and the instructor may wish to use his own demonstration dissection for this part of the work.

To remove the heart, cut through the postcava and the systemic, carotid, and pulmocutaneous arches on both sides. Now cut the pericardial attachments and remove the heart. Place the heart under water and trim away the walls of the atria and the ventricle with small scissors. You will probably find it convenient to do this under a dissecting microscope. After the interiors of the atria and the ventricle are exposed, insert one point of the scissors into the opening between the ventricle and the *bulbus cordis*. Make a ventral cut in the *bulbus cordis*, trimming the edges as necessary to expose the spiral valve and other structures. During your work refer to page 32.

To study the remaining portions of the circulatory system, it will be necessary to remove the liver and the alimentary canal. In removing the liver, it is important to avoid cutting the postcava. Lift the ventricle and identify the *sinus venosus* and the postcava. Starting at the anterior end of the liver on the right side, free the liver from the heart and lungs and remove the right lobe. If your specimen is a female, be careful to preserve the ostia of the oviducts during this operation. Similarly, remove the left lobes of the liver, keeping the postcava in sight and being careful to avoid it. Pick away the remaining portions of the liver which surround the postcava.

After removing the liver, cut the large intestine near the urinary bladder and then cut the mesentery to free the intestine and stomach. Cut the stomach near the esophagus and remove the stomach and intestine. Trim away the remaining portions of the mesentery and peritoneum to make a clean dissection of the kidneys, gonads, and related vessels. Identify the veins by referring to page 43. Cut the dorsolumbar vein and the peritoneum along the lateral edge of the right kidney, noting that the peritoneum in this area forms the ventral wall of the subvertebral lymph space. Lift the lateral edge of the right kidney and identify the arteries illustrated on page 35. Also see pages 36 through 40. Trace the arteries and veins of the pelvis and thigh by separating the surrounding muscles as necessary to expose the vessels illustrated.

Recently published papers on circulation and respiration in the frog do not always agree in their descriptions of the mechanisms involved. You may be interested in reading some of these studies, which are cited in the bibliography. Why is is that such apparently simple topics are not fully understood? What are some of the obstacles involved in the study of respiration and circulation in the living frog?

Study the diagrams on page 29 and be able to describe and compare circulation patterns in a typical fish, frog, and mammal. Of what significance is the evolutionary trend toward a reduction in the number of capillary systems through which blood passes before returning to the heart?

What is the function of the hepatic portal system? Of the renal portal system?

Assuming that during hibernation the frog depends entirely on cutaneous respiration, compare the approximate oxygen content of the blood as it passes through the following structures during (a) normal activity in warm weather, and (b) hibernation: left atrium, right atrium, ventricle, pulmocutaneous arch, systemic arch, carotid arch.

What disadvantages would the circulatory system of the frog have for a mammal? What disadvantages would the mammalian circulatory system have for a frog?

Compare the following statements:

"[In amphibians] blood . . . passes the heart twice in making a complete circuit of lungs and tissues, and arterial and venous blood are mixed. Physiologically speaking this is less efficient than the unmixed blood of the fish. It was a great advance in evolution for the amphibia to invade the land, but one of the penalties was this less efficient blood system."*

"In fishes above the cyclostome level . . . the blood passes through three . . . capillary systems, losing much pressure in each. . . . With the introduction of the lung circuit into the circulatory system and the abolition in adult amphibians of gill breathing, circulatory efficiency is greatly promoted. The gill capillary system is eliminated; hence all body tissues are reached arterially directly with little loss of pressure." (Romer)

Are the two authors using the same criteria in forming their estimates of the relative efficiency of the circulatory systems of fishes and amphibia? Can you think of any experiments by which an objective test of the relative efficiency of circulatory systems could be established?

De Graaf found that in *Xenopus laevis* "the body and head receive the most highly oxygenated blood, only scarcely contaminated with oxygen-poor blood from the right side [of the heart]." He also found that "the oxygen requirements of *Xenopus* may at times be extremely low. . . . It would appear, therefore, that when their lungs are functional, the blood contains more oxygen than is required in many circumstances." How can this finding be reconciled with the frequently encountered statement that the frog's circulatory system does not supply aerated blood to the body effectively? You may be interested in reading De Graaf's paper to find out how he estimated the oxygen requirements of *Xenopus*. He suggests that further research "should include investigation not only into the actual distribution patterns observed, but also into the mechanism whereby it is achieved, into the volume-flow relationships in the different blood vessels and vascular beds, and into the oxygen requirements of the tissues in different seasons."

The following statement appears in a current biology text: ". . . the frog heart represents a

transitional stage in the evolution of the double-pump heart."† But Foxon writes: ". . . there is no reason to regard the amphibian heart, as exemplified by the frog, as being in any way part of an ascending evolutionary series standing between that of fishes and higher tetrapods." Is one statement clearly true and the other clearly false, or do both perhaps require some modification? In what respects does the frog's heart probably resemble a stage in the evolution of the mammalian heart? In what respects is it probably a specialized structure?

THE UROGENITAL SYSTEM

Refer to pages 42 through 47. *111246*

Cut the pelvic veins and remove them together with the posterior portion of the ventral abdominal vein. Using a sharp scalpel, cut through the pelvic girdle in the midline and pull the legs back to expose the cloaca. Trace the Wolffian ducts and the neck of the urinary bladder to the points where they enter the cloaca. If your specimen is a female, attempt to find the point at which the ovisac joins the cloaca. This may be difficult due to the thinness of the ovisac and its collapsed condition in preserved specimens. Using a dissecting microscope, observe the nephrostomes, which appear as minute openings on the ventral surface of the kidney. Identify the structures illustrated on page 43 if your specimen is a male, or on page 44 if your specimen is a female.

Olmsted writes: "The final formulation of [Claude] Bernard's most important biological generalization was in these words: 'All the vital mechanisms, varied as they are, have only one object, that of preserving constant the conditions of life in the internal environment.'" Why is this considered Bernard's most important biological generalization? What role do the kidneys play in regulating the internal environment?

Briefly compare the functions of the following in excretion and/or respiration: skin, liver, lymph, blood, lungs, kidneys.

Describe the blood supply of the frog's kidney and compare it with that of the mammalian kidney.

Compare the courses of spermatozoa and urine in the frog and in man.

---

* Moore, John A. *Principles of Zoology* (New York: Oxford University Press, 1957).

† Johnson, Willis H., Richard A. Laubengayer and Louis E. DeLanney. *General Biology* (revised ed., New York: Holt, Rinehart and Winston, 1961).

What is the function of the nephrostomes in the adult frog? Are they found in the mammalian kidney? What role did they play in the evolution of the kidney?

Describe the seasonal variations in the fat bodies and the genital organs.

Describe the shape of the frog's ovary just before ovulation. What is the functional significance of its form? How does the shape of the frog's ovary compare with that of the human ovary?

Compare ovulation in the frog and in the human.

Swammerdam wrote: "I would fain know, by what art, regular motion, or contrivance an egg lying thus loosely in the body, can be conveyed into a narrow tube, whose opening is placed very high up near the heart? Certainly, the best thing we can do on this occasion, is to own such a conveyance utterly inconceivable by human understanding, and humbly acknowledge the narrow limits of our faculties." Why was Swammerdam, widely regarded as one of the keenest biological observers who ever lived, unable to discover the mechanism of egg transport in the frog?

Instructors who wish to prepare a demonstration of ovulation and egg transport in the frog will find instructions in *Experimental Embryology* by Roberts Rugh (rev. ed., Minneapolis: Burgess Publishing Co., 1948).

THE NERVOUS SYSTEM

Refer to pages 48 through 54.

Remove the skin from the dorsal surface of the eye, noting the nictitating membrane and the conjunctiva (the membrane attaching the inner surface of the lids to the sclera). Leave the tympanum intact. Starting in the midline, remove the muscles from the dorsal surface of the skull and vertebral column. Cut carefully to avoid damaging underlying structures and refer to a skeleton as you work. After obtaining a clean exposure of the skull and vertebral column, place the frog on its back in a dissecting pan containing enough 3 per cent nitric acid to fully cover the exposed bone. Leave the frog in the acid for about three days. This will dissolve out the mineral salts, reducing the skull and vertebral column to the consistency of cartilage.

Remove the frog from the acid bath and wash it in running water. Insert one point of your scissors into the *foramen magnum* and cut forward along the dorsal surface of the skull, using forceps and scissors as necessary to expose the brain. Now insert the point of your scissors into the vertebral canal and cut toward the hind legs to remove the dorsal surface of the vertebral column. This must be done very carefully. Make your cut shallow and work slowly, keeping the point of the scissors in view and being careful not to damage the spinal cord or nerves.

Before continuing you may wish to soak the frog in 5 per cent formalin for a day or two; this will harden the brain and spinal cord, making the rest of the dissection easier.

Using a dissecting microscope, remove the eye muscles and the roof of the nasal cavity on the right side. Chip away the auditory capsule and the right side of the skull until you can identify the structures illustrated on page 49.

Turn your specimen over and examine it from the ventral view to see the course of the spinal nerves along the dorsal body wall. Observe the calcareous bodies which surround the spinal nerves at their points of exit. Find the sympathetic trunks on either side of the vertebral column and notice their connections with the spinal nerves. Trace the branches of the sympathetic trunks to the viscera.

Turn the frog over so that the dorsal surface is toward you. Cut away the lateral portions of the vertebral column and trace the spinal nerves as illustrated on page 48. Observe the dorsal and ventral roots of the spinal nerves (see the diagram on page 11).

Now cut the olfactory nerves and gently raise the anterior part of the brain with small forceps, cutting the cranial nerves close to the skull. Continue working back in this way until the brain is completely free. Cut the spinal cord and remove the brain from the skull. Place the brain in a dish of water and examine it under a dissecting microscope. Identify as many of the cranial nerves as you can by referring to page 50.

Remove the eye by cutting the optic nerve and any remaining muscles. Place the eye in a dish of water and, working under a dissecting microscope, cut the eye in the vertical plane with small scissors. Do not attempt to cut the lens. Refer to page 52 and identify the structures illustrated.

In answering the following questions you may find it helpful to read chapter two of Gordon Walls's *Vertebrate Eye and Its Adaptive Radiation*, which contains an excellent summary of the basic facts of refraction and accommodation.

In frogs the lens moves away from the retina during accommodation. Basing your answer on this fact alone, would you expect the frog's eye at rest to be nearsighted (myopic), normalsighted (emmetropic), or farsighted (hypermetropic)? What kind of experiment could be devised to observe the movement of the lens during accommodation? What kind of experiment could be devised to test the visual acuity of the frog's eye at rest and during accommodation?

The following statements are found in books cited in the bibliography. Noble: "The [amphibian] eye at rest is moderately farsighted." Holmes: "In air the frog is myopic, or near-sighted." Walls: "These animals [frogs] are emmetropic in air." If you find conflicting statements in textbooks, how do you decide which statement is correct?

Walls writes: "Amphibians nearly all have a binocular field, wider in anurans than in urodeles . . ." This means that the frog sees objects directly ahead of it with both eyes simultaneously, and two images of the same object are transmitted to the brain. Romer says: "In such cases [binocular vision] the formation of two duplicate mental pictures seems an unnecessary procedure. Nevertheless, this is done, as far as can be discovered, in nonmammalian forms with overlapping visual fields." How could the truth of this statement be tested?

Romer says: "In land vertebrates light rays are bent as they enter the cornea, which consequently does much of the work of focusing. In fishes this is not the case, and the entire task is thus performed by the lens itself. In consequence, we find that the fish lens has a spherical shape, which gives it the highest resolving power." Are there any other factors which might make the spherical lens adapted to underwater vision?

Many nocturnal terrestrial animals have almost spherical lenses. Since the cornea does much of the work of focusing in air, what advantage does the spherical lens have for these animals?

In their paper *Refractive Error and Vision in Fishes,* Baylor and Shaw report considerable evidence, both from their own and other studies, to support the thesis that "most teleost fishes [are farsighted]. . . i.e., the focal length of the lens is too long and the image falls behind the retina." In what ways might farsightedness be an adaptive mechanism for underwater vision? Accommodation in teleosts is accomplished by moving the lens toward the retina. What happens, in a farsighted eye, when the lens moves toward the retina? Does the image become clearer or more blurred?

Compare the subjective visual experience of the frog and the human.

Bibliography

ANGEL, F. *Vie et Moeurs des Amphibiens*. Paris: Payout, 1947.

BAYLOR, EDWARD R. and EVELYN SHAW. 1962. *Refractive Error and Vision in Fishes*. Science, 136: 157–158.

COCHRAN, DORIS M. *Living Amphibians of the World*. Garden City: Doubleday, 1961.

CORTELYOU, J. R., A. HIBNER-OWERKO and J. MULROY. 1960. *Blood and Urine Calcium Changes in Totally Parathyroidectomized Rana pipiens*. Endocrinology, 66: 441–450.

CHERIAN, A. G. 1956. *The Mechanism of Respiration in the Frog*. Acta Physiol. et Pharmacol. Neerland, 5: 154–168.

ECKER, ALEXANDER. *The Anatomy of the Frog*. Translated, with annotations and additions, by George Haslam. Oxford: Clarendon Press, 1889.

ECKER, ALEXANDER, and ROBERT WIEDERSHEIM. *Anatomie des Frosches*. Revised by Ernst Gaupp. Braunschweig: Vieweg und Sohn, 1896–1904.

DE GRAFF, A. R. 1957 *Investigations into the Distribution of Blood in the Heart and Aortic Arches of Xenopus laevis (Daud.)*. J. Exp. Biol., 34: 143–172.

FOXON, G. E. H. 1951. *A Radiographic Study of the Passage of the Blood Through the Heart in the Frog and the Toad*. Proc. Zool. Soc. Lond., 121: 529–538.

GANS, CARL. 1961. *A Bullfrog and Its Prey*. Natural History, Vol 70, No. 2.

HOLMES, SAMUEL J. *The Biology of the Frog*. Fourth Edition. New York: Macmillan Company, 1934.

HAZELHOFF, E. H. 1952. *Die Trennung der Blutmassen mit verschiedenem Sauerstoffgehalt im Froschherzen*. Experientia, 8: 471.

HYMAN, LIBBIE H. *Comparative Vertebrate Anatomy*. Second Edition. Chicago: University of Chicago Press, 1942.

MARSHALL, A. MILNES. *The Frog; an Introduction to Anatomy, Histology and Embryology*. Twelfth Edition. London: Macmillan Company, 1928.

MARTIN, H. NEWELL. 1878. *The Normal Respiratory Movements of the Frog*. Jour. Physiol., 1: 131–170.

MOORE, JOHN A. (ed.). *Physiology of the Amphibia*. New York: Academic Press, 1964.

MUNTZ, W. R. A. *Vision in Frogs*. Scientific American. March, 1964.

NOBLE, G. KINGSLEY. *The Biology of the Amphibia*. New York: McGraw-Hill, 1931.

OLIVER, JAMES A. *The Natural History of North American Amphibians and Reptiles*. Princeton: D. Van Nostrand Co., 1955.

RUGH, ROBERTS. *The Frog, Its Reproduction and Development*. Philadelphia: Blakiston Co., 1951.

ROMER, ALFRED S. *The Vertebrate Body*. Philadelphia: W. B. Saunders Co. 1949.

SAVAGE, MAXWELL R. *The Ecology and Life History of the Common Frog*. London: Sir Isaac Pitman & Sons, 1961.

SHAPIRO, B. G. 1933. *The Topography and Histology of the Parathyroid Glandules in Xenopus laevis*. J. Anat., 68: 39.

Sharma, H. L. 1961. *Circulatory Mechanism in the Heart of a Frog, Rana pipiens*. J. Morph., 109 (3): 323–350.

SIMONS, J. R. 1959. *Distribution of the Blood from the Heart in Some Amphibia*. Proc. Zool. Soc. Lond., 132: 51–64.

TUMARKIN, 1955. *Evolution of the Auditory Conducting Apparatus*. Evolution, 9 (3): 221–243.

VANDERVAEL, F. 1933. *Recherches sur le Mechanism de la Circulation du Sang dans le Coeur des Amphibiens Anoures*. Arch. Biol., Paris, 44: 577–606.

WALLS, GORDON LYNN. *The Vertebrate Eye and Its Adaptive Radiation*. New York: Hafner Publishing Company, 1963.